The Scientific Basis
of the Art of Teaching

The Julius and Rosa Sachs Memorial Lectures
Teachers College, Columbia University
April 1977

THE
Scientific Basis
OF THE
Art of Teaching

N. L. GAGE
STANFORD UNIVERSITY

Teachers College Press
TEACHERS COLLEGE, COLUMBIA UNIVERSITY
NEW YORK & LONDON

This work was supported in part by funds from the National Institute of Education, U.S. Department of Health, Education, and Welfare, Contract No. NE-C-00-3-0061. The opinions expressed herein do not necessarily reflect the position, policy, or endorsement of the Institute.

Published 1978 by Teachers College Press
Teachers College, Columbia University
1234 Amsterdam Avenue
New York, N.Y. 10027

FOURTH PRINTING 1979

Library of Congress Cataloging in Publication Data

Gage, Nathaniel Lees, 1917–
   The scientific basis of the art of teaching.

   Bibliography: p.
   1. Teaching.   2. Educational research.   I. Title.
LB1025.G29   371.1'02   78-6250
ISBN 0-8077-2537-4

   Manufactured in the United States of America

To Lawrence A. Cremin

PREFACE

T HESE CHAPTERS are extensions of the three Julius and Rosa Sachs
Memorial Lectures that I was privileged to give at Teachers College,
Columbia University, in April 1977. They represent an attempt at setting
forth the field of research on teaching in ways that will be interesting to the
general reader and also useful to the research worker. For the general reader,
I hope that the thickets of jargon are scattered widely enough to permit a
reasonable and attractive journey. For the research worker, I hope that new
and promising ideas turn up at least occasionally.

The ideas in these lectures have obviously been developing in my
thinking over many years. Thus my friends and colleagues have had many
opportunities to contribute to both the broad outlines and the details of these
essays, and I am grateful to them for advice and encouragement on earlier
versions of the manuscript. They are David C. Berliner, Robert N. Bush,
John Crawford, Robert Crocker, Michael J. Dunkin, Gene V Glass, Garry
L. McDaniels, Wilbert J. McKeachie, Ingram Olkin, Barak Rosenshine,
Richard E. Schutz, Richard E. Snow, Robert S. Soar, Kent Viehoever, and
Philip H. Winne. They should be absolved, of course, of responsibility for
any shortcomings of this work.

My work was supported in part by funds from the National Institute of
Education, U.S. Department of Health, Education, and Welfare. The
opinions expressed in this publication do not necessarily reflect the position,
policy, or endorsement of the National Institute of Education.

I am indebted to the John Simon Guggenheim Memorial Foundation for
a fellowship that gave me the freedom to do this writing while on sabbatical
leave from Stanford University during the academic year 1976–1977. Also,
I am grateful to President Lawrence A. Cremin and the Trustees of Teachers
College, Columbia University, for the honor of serving as the Julius and
Rosa Sachs Visiting Professor of Psychology and Education at Teachers
College during the spring semester of 1977. To President Cremin I owe a
special debt for warm hospitality, generous understanding, and helpful

criticism. My temporary colleagues, especially Professors William G. Anderson, Samuel Ball, Arno A. Bellack, Leonard S. Blackman, R. Gary Bridge, Harold Cook, Joel R. Davitz, John F. Fanselow, Miriam L. Goldberg, Joseph C. Grannis, Elizabeth P. Hagen, Jean Pierre Jordaan, Dale Mann, Roger A. Myers, A. Harry Passow, Jonas F. Soltis, Abraham J. Tannenbaum, Wagner Thielens, Joanna P. Williams, and Richard M. Wolf, helped greatly in making Teachers College, especially the ninth floor of Thorndike Hall, a pleasant and stimulating place. I benefited particularly from the opportunity to meet with seminars led by Professors Bellack, Fanselow, and Goldberg. My stay was also enhanced by the many courtesies I received from Judy Suratt. Finally, I am grateful to Margaret B. Gage in a thousand ways.

N. L. GAGE

Stanford, California

CONTENTS

The Scientific Basis
of the Art of Teaching

CHAPTER I

Reviewing What We Know: The Results of Recent Research

A T THE OUTSET, we should celebrate for a moment the importance of
what lies behind the abstraction called teaching. What I am talking
about is what a parent is concerned with — what you yourself may have experienced on the day you left your first child at his or her first school. As you
walked away from the classroom door, having put your daughter or son into
the hands of that stranger called the teacher, you appreciated with something
approaching adequate intensity the importance of what teachers do. That
appreciation ought properly to continue with only slight diminution through
all the years in which contact with teachers continues. For teachers can make
education a thing of joy and success or a matter of frustration and despair.

Teaching also looms large at the societal level. Since 1971, this country
has spent more money on education than on national defense. In 1975, 7.9
percent of our gross national product was spent on education while only 5.5
percent was spent on defense (Golladay, 1977, p. 16). And the largest single
item in our education budget was salaries for our two million full-time
elementary and secondary school teachers. That fact alone signalizes the
importance of teachers. No other kind of person has more effect on the success of what goes on in our schools.

As a topic, "the scientific basis of the art of teaching" seems to cry out
for some definitions. The terms *art, teaching,* and *scientific basis* need to be
pinned down at least briefly before we can proceed. Even if I cannot do full
justice to these definitions here, simply because these matters run long and
deep and properly belong to philosophers (see, for example, Hart, 1976), I
should set forth the particular conceptions that I have in mind.

What Is "Teaching"?

By *teaching* I mean any activity on the part of one person intended to facilitate learning on the part of another. Although the activity often involves language, it need not do so, nor need teaching rely solely on rational and intellectual processes. We can teach by providing silent demonstrations for our students or models for them to imitate. And we often teach by fostering attitudes and appreciations whose rational components are suffused with affect.

Teaching can proceed by many different methods, old and new. These methods can be grouped according to the number of students being taught at one time. So, for one student at a time, we have tutoring, seatwork, and computer-assisted instruction. For 2 to 20 students at a time, we have discussion methods, role playing, simulations, and games. For groups of say 40 or more students, we have lectures, films, television, and radio. And for groups numbering between 20 and 40, and averaging about 30, which is the typical class size in our elementary and secondary schools, we have classroom teaching. This method incorporates many of the other methods but also includes a procedure fairly distinctive to itself — one called classroom recitation. Because classroom teaching is by far the most prevalent method in our schools, it is the one I shall be concerned with here.

Thus I shall not deal with comparisons *between* methods — for example, comparisons between lecture and discussion, programmed instruction and television, the so-called personalized system of instruction and conventional courses. Rather, I want to compare different styles of classroom teaching, that is, to make *within*-method comparisons in which different teacher and pupil behaviors within classroom teaching have been studied. This seems to me to be, at least for the near future, the most useful kind of study, because large-scale, radical departures from classroom teaching are still at least decades away. (See, for example, the symposium edited by Cunningham, 1977.) Even when these new methods finally arrive, they will not completely displace classroom teaching.

We can conceive of a continuum with votaries of a humanistic *art* of teaching at one end. This art rejects the offerings and findings of those who seek to apply scientific method to the improvement of teaching. At the other end are believers in the replacement of teachers by *technology*, in the form of teaching machines, computer-assisted instruction, multimedia packages, and the like. Our present concern with the scientific basis of the art of classroom teaching belongs near the middle of this range.

What Is "Art"?

Now let us turn to the questions of what is an art, and how can teaching be a form of art. Teaching is, of course, a useful, or practical, art rather than one dedicated to the creation of beauty and the evocation of aesthetic pleasure as ends in themselves. As a practical art, teaching must be recognized as a process that calls for intuition, creativity, improvisation, and expressiveness — a process that leaves room for departures from what is implied by rules, formulas, and algorithms. In teaching, by whatever method it proceeds — even in the fixed programs of computer-assisted instruction — there is a need for artistry: in the choice and use of motivational devices, clarifying definitions and examples, pace, redundancy, and the like.

When teaching goes on in face-to-face interaction with students, the opportunity for artistry expands enormously. No one can ever prescribe successfully all the twists and turns to be taken as the lecturer, the discussion leader, or the classroom teacher uses judgment, sudden insight, sensitivity, and agility to promote learning.

Although teaching has long been termed an art, the usage has generally been metaphorical. As an approach to understanding and evaluating teaching, the critical study of the art of teaching has received little serious attention. Recently, however, Eisner (1977) has suggested that the same connoisseurship and criticism be applied to classroom life that have been applied to other art forms. Such an application, as a supplement to the scientific methods I am discussing, would exploit the same kinds of intellectual and perceptual apparatus — the study of holistic qualities rather than analytically derived quantities, the use of "inside" rather than externally objective points of view — that have been developed for the criticism of literature, the visual arts, and music. An example can be seen in the study of the human face. No quantitative scheme of physical measurement has yet succeeded in specifying what makes a face beautiful or plain. The connoisseurs and critics refuse to be stopped by that fact. They use their ability to perceive integrated patterns of features to appreciate, describe, and judge faces — and classrooms — relying on their accumulated experience, cultural backgrounds, and evocative language to grapple with the task of understanding, responding, and evaluating.

One of Eisner's students, Greer (1973), making much use of Pepper's *Basis of Criticism in the Arts* (1945), has pursued the criticism of teaching to the point of showing what such a nonscientific yet disciplined and rational examination of teaching as an art form would lead to. Was the lesson enjoyable in the sense of presenting information appealing to the various senses, using metaphor to enrich connotations, creating excitement and tension? Was the pervasive quality of the experience in the lesson related to life? Was the tension creatively resolved? Was the lesson appropriately related to others taught by this teacher?

In a sense, none of these questions is answerable only through the sensibilities of the connoisseur and critic. If the behavioral scientist has no monopoly of serious concern with teaching, neither has the aesthetician. Eisner properly holds that connoisseurship "might provide new subject matters . . . for conventional empirical research" (p. 351). But the empirical research can also enlighten the connoisseur as to "important things about life in the classroom" (p. 350). The correlations of types of teacher behavior with what pupils learn and feel can guide the connoisseur as much as the connoisseur can guide the scientist.

Both approaches can be concerned with many of the same aspects of teaching, but in different ways. Behavioral scientists attempt to translate these aspects into "low-inference" variables, that is, characteristics or behaviors that are as explicitly and directly observable as possible. They thus convert "warmth" into, say, the frequency with which the teacher smiles, praises and, in the primary grades, hugs. In so doing, they gain unambiguity and an idea of what behaviors teachers should change if their warmth is to change. But they also risk losing the essence of warmth.

Aestheticians, on the other hand, would leave the percept *warmth* in its holistic, high-inference form — with all its implicit richness and significance. In doing so, they are required to infer teacher warmth from an ineffable congeries of events in the classroom, and they may be hard put to tell anyone else just what determined these global impressions. The aesthetician gains the advantage of dealing with an unquestionably significant feature of classroom life but pays the price of needing to be vague and metaphorical when it comes to telling anyone just what he or she should do in order to become more or less warm. The same would apply to most other high-inference, "qualitative" (rather than "quantitative") phenomena, such as clarity, enthusiasm, and vividness. It is easy to tell teachers to be clear, but only a translation of clarity into low-inference behaviors permits us to tell teachers just what they should do to become clear.

In short, teaching as an art can become the object of the same kind of perceptive scholarship that is devoted to other art forms. But we are here concerned with the scientific basis of that art.

What Is a "Scientific Basis"?

Almost no one will argue with what I have said thus far — that variations within classroom teaching are worth studying and that teaching, especially in its socially interactive forms, must entail some artistry. But what about the idea of a scientific basis for the art of teaching? Here I step onto controversial ground, and it is on that ground that this essay takes its stand.

Let me begin by distinguishing between a science of teaching and a scientific basis for the art of teaching: The former idea, a science of teaching, claims much more and is in the end, I think, erroneous. It implies that good teaching will some day be attainable by closely following rigorous laws that yield high predictability and control. For example, when the chemist uses available knowledge, he or she practices science, not art, to obtain almost completely predictable results, as specific elements and compounds are brought together under certain conditions. But when scientists are doing research, they are themselves practicing an art. A recent experiment in which the charge of an electron was measured to an accuracy of two parts in 10 billion was described as an "experimental work of art." Here the scientist does use judgment, intuition, and insight in handling the unpredicted — contingencies of the same kind that arise when a painting, a poem, or a pupil is the target of an artistic effort.

Practical enterprises, those conducted in the real world rather than in the laboratory, have both artistic and scientific components. The practice of medicine provides an example. In the twentieth century, medicine's scientific basis, however incomplete, is undeniable. The physician works with a thousand variables that have been identified and related to other variables by scientific methods. Body temperature, red cell count, cholesterol content, blood pressure, respiration rate—these few variables that even laymen recognize—have acquired their medical significance from scientific methods. But the physician uses the variables in what must be considered an artistic way as he approaches each new patient. Arthur Elstein, a psychologist who has collaborated in major projects dealing with physicians' thought processes, has defined *clinical* as "any of the artful, informal, qualitative or not explicitly quantitative strategies generally employed by clinicians" for the task of reaching diagnostic decisions (1976, p. 696).

One could present a similar portrayal of how the engineer works. Engineers, too, have a strong scientific foundation, usually in physics and chemistry. But in their practical work of solving problems in the design of bridges, engines, or communication systems, they also rely on artistry as they balance the claims of competing considerations. An electrical engineer, Cravens Wanlass, describing what he did in the course of inventing a revolutionary energy-saving electric motor, said:

> People think you sit down with a calculator and just run through the equations and come up with something. . . . It doesn't work like that. It's almost a creative process, like art or music (*Washington Post*, May 9, 1977, p. A6).

My analogy is obvious. In medicine and engineering, where the scientific basis is unquestionable, the artistic elements also abound. In teaching, where the artistic elements are unquestionable, a scientific base can also be developed. These professions are not in themselves sciences; they merely have scientific bases. To practice medicine and engineering requires a knowledge of much science: concepts, or variables, and their interrelations in the form of strong or weak laws, generalizations, or trends. But using the science to achieve practical ends requires artistry — the artistry that enters into knowing when to follow the implications of the laws, generalizations, and trends, and, especially, when *not* to, and how to combine two or more laws or trends in solving a problem.

In practical affairs, the laws and trends relating any two variables are subject to modification by the influence of third variables and many more variables. These influences of third and additional variables are called interactions. When any additional variable interacts to influence the relationship between two variables, we are unwise to follow the implications of a simple two-variable relationship. For example, the relationship between teacher criticism and pupil achievement may be negative for pupils with lower academic orientation and positive for pupils with higher academic orientation (Crawford & Gage, 1977). Here the relationship between the first two variables (teacher criticism and pupil achievement) is influenced by the value of a third (pupil's degree of academic orientation).

Some writers have responded to the fact of such interactions by concluding that they make practical applications of relationships well-nigh impossible. But the behavioral sciences, including research on teaching, are no worse off in this respect than are the natural sciences. In physics, for example, many relationships are about as firm as anyone could wish. Yet, considered one at a time, these relationships hold only under laboratory conditions and not in real life. When it comes to real-life phenomena, physical scientists must apply many of those laws in combination. Only one example need be cited: what might be called the interactions that complicate the motion of, say, a flare released from the mast of a moving ship. First, the motion can be resolved into horizontal and vertical components, but this is

> only the first step in an essentially infinite chain of resolutions. If one wants more detail about the motion, other laws enter. The appearance of the Coriolis force is responsible for an eastward deflection of the object. The laws for falling bodies in real media at various Reynolds numbers have to enter to calculate the effect of friction and turbulence. The more detail one wants to know, the more resolutions become necessary (Holton, 1975, p. 330).

Thus, even the apparently simple laws of mechanics interact with a host of other laws. But physical scientists do not denigrate their main effects simply because interaction effects also occur. They simply take more laws into account.

Gergen (1973) has made the point that laws, or generalizations, in the behavioral and social sciences tend to change as time goes on. The laws rest on values concerning what is desirable and important, and those values, being learned, are changeable. Even the learning process depends on reinforcers whose potency is learned. Thus, the law of reinforcement changes as different stimuli (e.g., social approval) become stronger or weaker as reinforcers. Even more important, "knowledge of the theory enables one to avoid being ensnared by its prediction" (p. 316). People who know about the laws can easily evade them. Knowing that one is being praised in order to improve one's participation may make the praise ineffective.

Such possible failures of behavioral laws to have "transhistorical validity" need not concern students of teaching in any culture whose values are shared by the influencers and the influenced. Suppose the teacher, the pupil, and the pupil's parents want a pupil to learn to read or to understand the Pythagorean theorem. Then the pupil's knowledge that the teacher is trying to facilitate such learning should not lead the pupil to subvert the teacher's effort. When the teacher uses scheduled drill, a clarifying explanation, or reinforcing tokens, it is unlikely that the pupils' desire to escape to freedom will lead them deliberately to undo what the teacher has done. The results of research on teaching may not last eternally, but they should last long enough to have practical value in any given generation.

Thus we see that the relationships between teacher behavior variables and what students learn should be applied with due regard for other factors, such as the ability and anxiety level of the pupils, the objectives of teaching, the characteristics of various pupils in the class, or the specific task to be taught at any given moment. Whenever those interacting factors are shown to be important, we can use the interactions along with whatever main effects are at hand. The general relationships that teachers work with must be combined in complex ways as adaptations are made to the particulars of any specific problem.

Scientific method can contribute relationships between variables taken two at a time and even, in the form of interactions, three or perhaps four or more at a time. Beyond say four, the usefulness of what science can give the teacher begins to weaken, because teachers cannot apply, at least not without help and not on the run, the more complex interactions. At this point, the teacher as artist must step in and make clinical, or artistic, judgments about the best ways to teach. In short, the scientific base for the art of teaching will consist of two-variable relationships and lower-order interactions. The higher-order interactions between four and more variables must be handled by the teacher as artist.

Is such a scientific basis, admittedly limited to simpler relationships, worth having? The answer is yes; it is better to have generalizations to which exceptions can be made than to have no generalizations at all. Josiah Royce, the Harvard philosopher, put it well in 1891 when he wrote that

> it is vain that the inadequacy of science is made a sufficient excuse for knowing nothing of it. The more inadequate science is when alone, the more need of using it as a beginning when we set about our task. . . . Instinct needs science, not as a substitute, but as a partial support. . . . [W]hen you teach, you must know when to forget formulas; but you must have learned them in order to be able to forget them (Royce, 1891, in Borrowman, 1965, pp. 112–113).

REQUISITES FOR A SCIENTIFIC BASIS

What does it mean to say that some field of practice, such as the art of teaching, has a scientific basis? The answer must again be put simply here. As I have already intimated, a scientific basis consists of knowledge of regular, nonchance relationships in the realm of events with which the practice is concerned. The relationships need not be perfect or even close to perfect. Rather, the relationships need merely be better than those that would occur by chance. In the statistician's terms, this means that correlations should be different from zero — not plus one or minus one, but different from zero. And, as everyone knows, the difference from zero should be statistically significant rather than a mere chance departure from zero.

Sometimes even very weak relationships can be important. As shown in Table 1, the correlation between cigarette smoking and lung cancer was only .14 in the study reported by Lilienthal, Pedersen, and Dowd (1967, p. 78). Yet, on the basis of such correlations, important public health policy has been made and millions of persons have changed strong habits. And the coefficient of .14 is somewhat lower in magnitude than that which might be found for any single variable of teacher behavior in relation to pupil achievement.

TABLE 1

Frequency of Smoking in Lung Cancer Patients
and Matched Controls

	Patients with lung cancer	Matched patients with other diseases	Total
Number of smokers	499	462	961
Number of nonsmokers	19	56	75
Total	518	518	1036

phi coefficient = .14*

SOURCE: Based on data in Lilienthal et al. (1967, p. 78).

*Even phi/phi max, where the coefficient is related to its maximal value for any combination of marginal proportions, is only .45, which is no larger than the correlation often obtained between single variables in teacher behavior and adjusted mean achievement of the teachers' classes.

Types of Relationships between Variables

The kind of science that has occupied the mainstream of educational research over the last 50 years involves relationships between variables. Let me remind you of what such relationships look like in the realm of teaching. We can have *predictive* relationships, and we can have *causal* relationships.

For instance, we would predict that children will score higher on achievement tests at the end of the year if they have spent more time acquiring the knowledge, understandings, and skills measured by those achievement tests. Thus we can predict that children who spend about 5,000 minutes per school year on appropriate reading tasks — tasks that are relevant and not too hard or easy — will do better in reading at the end of the year than those who spend only about 3,000 minutes per year on reading. Therefore, we have here a predictive relationship.

But what about control or improvement? For that purpose, we need a causal relationship. It may be that the predictive relationship does not really reflect a causal relationship. Perhaps the children who are better at reading to begin with, who have more talent for it, simply tend to do more reading. In that event, the amount of time spent on reading is the effect rather than the cause of reading achievement. We determine causal relationships, of course, by the kind of controlled experiment in which we manipulate the amount of time spent on reading. That would mean picking some children at random from all our children and simply arranging, through assignments and classroom management, for them to spend more time at reading than the remaining children who have been assigned to the lower amount of time on reading. Now, if we find a difference in reading achievement at the end of the year, we can safely conclude that a cause-and-effect relationship exists: more time spent on reading causes, or brings about, higher achievement.

In short, our scientific basis must consist of established relationships between variables in teaching and learning. We need reliable correlation coefficients, or differences between averages, or similar statistics.

Types of Variables

Now I should like to touch upon the kinds of variables that would be involved in a scientific basis for the art of teaching. These have been classified by Mitzel (1960) and by Dunkin and Biddle (1974) in a kind of time sequence. At the beginning we have so-called *presage* variables — certain teacher characteristics such as age, sex, social class background, and training experiences.

At about the same point in the sequence we also find *context* variables. These are the grade level, subject matter, size of class, type of community, and other features of the context within which the teaching and learning take place. Before any teaching method can be specified, it is necessary to know, at least roughly, two major aspects of this context. First we need to know the objectives of our teaching — at least the subject matter and, if possible, the kinds of knowledge, understanding, attitude, sensibility, or skill that the learner is to be helped to acquire. Second, we need to know something about our students — at least their age level and, if possible, something about what they already know, understand, and feel about the subject matter and themselves.

After the presage and context variables come the *process* variables, those that describe what goes on in the teaching–learning situation. These variables deal with the ways in which the teachers and pupils behave and interact — think, feel, talk, write, move, and relate to one another. This is the realm of teaching methods and styles.

Finally, we come to the *product* or *outcome* variables, which denote the amount of learning, or achievement of educational objectives. How well can the pupils read at the end of the school year? How well do they like reading? How well do they like themselves? These questions, and dozens like them, refer to the outcomes of the presage and process variables operating in a given context.

With four types of variables we can conceive of six possible pairings of the types and thus six possible kinds of relationships between pairs of variables of these types: context–process, context–product, presage–process, presage–product, context–presage, and process–product. Many studies have indeed been made of presage–process or context–process and the other four kinds of relationships (see Dunkin & Biddle, 1974). Further, much effort has been expended on the study of process occurrence in itself. Just what goes on in classrooms is intriguing in its own right, as witnessed by the detailed studies of language in the classroom by Arno Bellack and his coworkers (1966). This kind of work is flourishing, especially in studies by ethnographers, sociologists, and linguists.

But these six kinds of relationships among our four kinds of variables do not occupy an equal position in the eyes of those who want to improve teaching — teachers, teacher educators, parents, and school adminstrators. What they want to know about — especially those who are interested in a scientific basis for the art of teaching — are process–product relationships. They want to know whether the teacher's thinking, behaving, acting — in short, teaching — in one way is demonstrably better in terms of some values or purposes than teaching in another way. If the answer is yes, we have a basis for improving teaching and the training of teachers. If the answer is no, we are left without a scientific basis for the art of teaching. Then every teacher must use his or her personal common sense, intuition, insight, or art, with no guidance from any relationships or regularities that may have been laid bare through scientific methods.

NEGATIVE VIEWS ON THE PROCESS-PRODUCT EVIDENCE

So far, what I have had to say has been altogether elementary, however necessary to lay the basis for my argument. But I am now entering into matters on which most writers' conclusions over the years have been negative; mine and some others' (e.g., Good, Biddle, & Brophy, 1975; Rosenshine, 1976) are positive. Most reviewers have concluded their reports by saying that past work has been essentially fruitless. Such discouraging characterizations of previous findings go back at least 25 years (see, for example, Committee on the Criteria of Teacher Effectiveness, 1952) and are still being repeated in present-day publications.

Examples from Recent Writers

For example, in 1978 Doyle asserted that "Reviewers have concluded, with remarkable regularity, that few consistent relationships between teacher variables and effectiveness criteria can be established" [nine reviews cited] (p. 164). Similarly, Shavelson and Dempsey (1976) began by noting that the research has not "identified consistent, replicable features of human teaching that lead directly — or even indirectly — to valued student outcomes" (p. 553). These conclusions may be questioned — and have been questioned recently — on many grounds.

Negative reviewers have found fault with a variety of design and analysis features of the research. For example, Heath and Nielson (1974) criticized the studies for failing to use random assignment of pupils to treatments, although classrooms rather than pupils are the proper unit of analysis and, in any case, such random assignment would fly in the face of the realities of school organization. Heath and Nielson also faulted the studies for omitting tests of the assumptions of various statistical techniques (such assumptions as normality, homogeneity of variance, and linearity). Yet, as Hedges (1978) has pointed out in detail, failure to test these assumptions did not, in all likelihood, impair seriously the validity of the studies. The same is true, from my viewpoint, of the Heath–Nielson criticisms relative to types of covariance adjustment, tests for parallel slopes of regression planes, and tests for detecting outliers in the data.

Glass (1976) has recognized that "a study with a half dozen design and analysis flaws may still be valid. . . . It is an empirical question whether relatively poorly designed studies give results significantly at variance with those of the best designed studies" (p. 4). Glass's own impression is that the difference in results between well-designed and poorly designed experiments is "so small that to integrate research results by eliminating the 'poorly' done studies is to discard a vast amount of important data" (p. 6). This impression is borne out by Stickell's critical review of the methodology and results of research comparing televised and face-to-face instruction (cited in Taveggia, 1974, p. 403). Comparisons were rated as "interpretable" ($N = 10$), "partially interpretable" ($N = 23$), and "uninterpretable" ($N = 217$) on the basis of their design and statistical procedures. The three groups of studies agreed in suggesting the same conclusion, namely, that there was no difference in the academic achievement of students taught by the two methods. Similarly, Yin, Bingham, and Heald (1976) concluded that there was "a general lack of relationship between quality [of evaluation studies] and the outcomes of the innovative experience" (pp. 153-154).

The Main Error: Maximizing Risks of Type II Errors

I want to concentrate on what I consider to be another major error underlying the many dismal summations I have mentioned. This error can be illustrated by reference to a volume that, although altogether praiseworthy for its thoroughness and clarity in organizing the field, commits what I consider to be the same serious error as all its predecessors.

I am referring to the volume by Dunkin and Biddle (1974) entitled *The Study of Teaching*. These authors brought together into clusters all the studies they considered to bear upon a given dimension of teacher behavior. Then Dunkin and Biddle summarized the findings of these clusters of studies in statements such as the following:

> Teacher "indirectness" is *unrelated* to pupil achievement [and here they cite 15 correlational studies and go on to say that] In contradiction, *it is also found that* . . . Higher teacher "indirectness" *is associated with* greater pupil achievement [and here they cite 10 correlational studies] (p. 115).

("Teacher indirectness" refers, of course, to the well-known concept derived by Ned Flanders from his interaction analysis categories. Such indirectness "consists of soliciting the opinions and ideas of pupils, applying and enlarging on those opinions and ideas, praising or encouraging the participation of pupils, and accepting their feelings" [Flanders, 1967, p. 109].) Thus it would appear from the Dunkin–Biddle summary that the score is 15 to 10 against the significance of teacher indirectness for pupil achievement. The Dunkin–Biddle descriptions of the findings of many other clusters of process–product studies typically conclude with statements giving the by now familiar impression that research on teaching has yielded almost completely equivocal, nonsignificant, and inconsistent findings.

How did Dunkin and Biddle and the many writers who agree with them arrive at these conclusions? Dunkin and Biddle cited no quantitative results, statistical measures, or levels of significance. They describe their reviewing method as entailing an examination (and correction, if necessary) of each investigation and its claims. "In short, our procedures involved clinical judgments, made use of multiple criteria, and were based primarily on the criterion of statistical significance" (p. 453). But, by basing their clinical judgment primarily on the statistical significance, or nonattributability to chance, of the results of single studies, they risk committing to a large degree what statisticians call an error of Type II, that is, an error of considering a relationship or difference to be nonexistent when it does in fact exist.

On what reasoning can this charge against the Dunkin–Biddle procedure be based? First, it seems safe to assume that the true relationship, if any, between any single dimension of teacher behavior and pupil achievement or attitude is probably low. It would be surprising indeed if any single variable, such as teacher "indirectness," by itself had a high correlation with, or accounted for any substantial portion of the variance in, student achievement or attitude. On the face of it, the teaching–learning process is so complex that any single significant variable in teacher behavior should have only a low correlation (ranging from about $\pm .1$ to about $\pm .4$) with student achievement or attitude.

Second, the types of studies of teaching with which we are concerned are typically based on relatively small numbers of teachers. Thus, in 19 studies of the relationship between teacher indirectness and student achievement, as brought together by Dunkin and Biddle (p. 115), the number of teachers involved ranged from 8 to 70, with a median of 15. Only 5 of the 19 studies used samples consisting of more than 18 teachers.

Third, for a sample of that median size, namely 15 teachers, it is necessary that a correlation coefficient equal .51 if it is to be significant at the .05 level, that is, have only 5 chances in 100 of arising by chance when the true correlation is zero. The coefficent must equal .64 if it is to be significant at the .01 level.

What can we conclude in view of these sample sizes and our expectations concerning the magnitude of the relationships between single dimensions of teaching behavior and student achievement or attitude? To my mind, it seems evident that most of the single studies should not be expected to yield statistically significant results. Thus, with such sample sizes, we shall almost never reject the null hypothesis (the hypothesis that the true correlation is zero) even when it is false.

More Valid Ways of Reviewing the Evidence

What can be done in a field of research where sample sizes are small and expected correlations and differences are also small? Is it possible to extract useful knowledge from such studies?

Vote Counting

One attempt to do so was recently made by McKeachie and Kulik (1975) in comparing the lecture and discussion methods of college teaching. Going beyond a previous review by Dubin and Taveggia (1968), one that had considered only the mean score on the final examination, McKeachie and Kulik considered three types of criteria — a "factual examination," a measure of "retention and higher level thinking," and measures of "attitudes and motivation." For each study reviewed, they tallied whether the lecture or the discussion method was superior, with statistical significance disregarded. This kind of vote counting yielded impressive consistencies. In 21 comparisons on the "factual examination," the lecture method was superior in 12, about equal to the discussion method in 4, and inferior to the discussion method in 5. In 7 comparisons on "retention and higher level thinking," the discussion method was superior in all 7. In 9 comparisons on desirable "attitudes and motivation," the discussion method was superior in 7, tied in 1, and inferior in 1.

The "Unknowability" Argument

At this point we should consider what might be termed the "unknowability" argument. This is the argument that negative, or nonsignificant, findings tend to remain unpublished and that to conduct a vote count "is to tabulate from a biased sample" (Dunkin & Biddle, 1974, p. 453). Many research workers seem to be impressed by this argument on the basis of personal experience or anecdotal evidence. They claim to know of at least one study that was never published because it yielded negative or non-significant results.

The abundance of nonsignificant findings in the literature of research on teaching certainly calls the point into question, however. Furthermore, the possibility has been investigated. It was indeed found by Sterling (1959) and Bozarth and Roberts (1972), in a survey of hundreds of research articles, that about 95 percent of those that used tests of statistical significance reported a finding that was statistically significant at the .05 level at least. But Hunt (1975) counted tests of significance rather than articles. He found that, of the first five articles in one issue of the *Journal of Experimental Psychology,* three reported tests of significance. Of the 110 tests in those three articles, only 29 percent were significant at the .05 level or better. Hunt concluded that "it cannot be said that only significant findings are published" (p. 592). That published tests of significance are significant more than 5 percent of the time at the .05 level should simply indicate that research workers tend to seek and test relationships that are suggested by good scientific reasoning.

Finally, Glass (1976), in his comparison of the results of published studies and those of unpublished studies (such as dissertations) in the field of psychotherapy, found only a slightly greater effect size in the published studies:

> studies published in books showed an average effect size of $.8\sigma_x$; studies from journals had a mean effect size of $.7\sigma_x$; thesis studies averaged $.6\sigma_x$; and unpublished studies averaged $.5\sigma_x$. The tendency to place the more favorable findings in the more prestigious outlets is clearly present, but the situation is nowhere as bad as we once cynically imagined (p. 42).

The implication is that, in psychotherapy research at least, there is no powerful tendency to withhold publication of nonsignificant or negative findings.

My final point on this matter is that the unknowability argument jeopardizes forever any conclusions based on available evidence. No matter how consistent and significant the published results may be, they can never refute definitively the argument that even more nonsignificant or negative findings have gone unpublished. We have here a "principle of unknowability" that reduces to futility any effort to accumulate evidence and draw conclusions in the behavioral sciences.

Thus I set the unknowability argument aside and turn to an improvement on vote counting, especially when that technique is based on the statistical significance of single studies, as in the collations by Dunkin and Biddle — collations that led to the conclusions I have already mentioned.

Testing the Significance of Combined Results

The improvement I propose takes into account the size of the sample and the magnitude of the relationship or difference. It consists of testing the significance of *combined* results by a method attributed by Jones and Fiske (1953) to Karl and Egon Pearson. This technique entails converting the exact probability value of the result of any single study into a value of the statistic called chi square. Then the values of chi square are summed over studies, and the significance, or probability, of the sum is determined. In essence, the technique provides an estimate of the statistical significance, or "nonchanceness," of the whole cluster of independent findings that are considered by the research reviewer to deal with a specified process variable, or aspect of teacher behavior or teaching method. Rather than relying on the weak single studies based on small samples, we can use this technique to gain the greater statistical power of a cluster of studies bearing on the same relationship.

What happens when this method of appraising results is used? With the help of a research assistant, Dale Schunk, I have applied the chi-square model to four clusters of studies that had been formed by Dunkin and Biddle (1974) — clusters that I have accepted as the basis for the present argument.

For each study we could use only one result. Thus, when there was more than one result in a given study, we used the weakest one to obtain a most conservative estimate and the mean of the results to obtain an estimate of the average significance of the study.

One cluster, shown in Table A in the Appendix, included 19 studies of the relationship between *teacher indirectness* and student achievement. When the most conservative combination of the usable results of 16 of these studies was tested, as shown in Table B, it proved to be highly significant, indicating that this set of results could have occurred by chance less than once in a thousand times.

A second cluster of studies, shown in Table C, dealt with the frequency of *teacher praise* in relation to pupil attitudes. Here the combined results of five correlational studies, also shown in Table C, was significant at better than the .10 level.

A third cluster, shown in Table D, consisted of eight studies of *teacher acceptance of pupil ideas* in relation to pupil achievement. As shown in Table E, when the most conservative estimate was made, by using only the weakest results of the studies that yielded more than one result, the test of the significance of the combined results indicated a relationship that could have occurred by chance less than once in a hundred times.

Finally, for our fourth cluster, shown in Table F, we had 17 studies of the relationship between *teacher criticism and disapproval,* on the one hand, and pupil achievement, on the other. Here, as shown in Table G, the most conservative combination of results, most of which were *negative* correlations, was significant at the .10 level, while the combination of mean results of the 17 studies was significant at better than the .001 level.

These findings mean that research on teaching has indeed yielded some statistically significant, or nonchance, clusters of results. Considered as clusters, the studies acquire sufficient power to dispel the false impression created when the statistical significance of weak single studies is taken seriously. These results, based on the first four attempts to apply the chi-square model to the clusters of studies that are available in the literature, suggest that we may now rid ourselves of the pessimism about process–product relationships so often expressed in previous characterizations of the literature. We do have some relationships between teacher behavior and pupil achievement and attitudes on which a scientific basis for the art of teaching may be erected.

Results Obtained by Glass and His Coworkers

But statistically significant results from clusters of studies mean merely that the correlation or difference is probably greater than zero. We immediately begin to wonder, How much greater? Glass, Coulter, Hartley, Hearold, Kahl, Kalk, and Sherretz (1977) determined that the cluster of 19 studies of teacher indirectness, shown in Table A of the Appendix, yields results that have a mean value in correlational terms of about .25. Glass and his coworkers were able to make this estimate because Glass (1978) has developed techniques for converting into correlation coefficients a wide variety of other statistics, such as t ratios, F ratios, chi squares, and Mann–Whitney Us.

Hence it was possible for Glass and his coworkers (1977) to average the correlation coefficients thus obtained separately for the elementary school grades and the secondary school grades. They found that the average coefficient for the eight secondary school studies was about .30 and for the ten elementary school studies only about .15. This grade-level difference in the importance of teacher indirectness seems consistent, as we shall see, with the general picture of effective teaching in the primary grades, as that picture has emerged from a number of major studies and reviews of the research literature.

Major Studies and Reviews of Teaching in the Early Grades

Let us turn now to the findings of recent studies of teaching in the early elementary school grades. The research at this level has been far more adequate and extensive than that at the secondary school level — largely, as Medley (1977) has pointed out, because of the Federal government's funding policies. These policies have focused effort on the improvement of teaching in the early grades, as in the massive studies of Project Follow Through.

The research available for synthesis is similar in many respects to that in other areas studied by behavioral scientists, such as counseling, psychotherapy, or the effects of television on children. There are few if any unflawed studies. Yet, if the studies tend to yield the same implications from many different approaches, our confidence in those implications can be maintained.

Before we proceed, we should note the difference between two methods of research. The first compares intact patterns of teaching, such as direct and open styles. This method studies the relationship between these patterns of teaching and what pupils learn. The second method deals with many specific dimensions, or variables, of teaching styles or methods. Here the investigators study the relationships between each of hundreds of variables within various teaching styles and what pupils learn. From the hundreds of correlations, especially the significant ones, the investigators and reviewers then synthesize the style or pattern of teaching that seems to be associated with desirable kinds of pupil achievement and attitude. In what follows, we shall consider the yield of each of these kinds of studies in turn.

Comparisons of Direct and Open Teaching

First, we have the comprehensive study by Traub, Weiss, Fisher, Musella, and Khan (1973). They compared results in open and closed schools in Canada, also distinguishing between schools with relatively few students for whom English was a second language (Type I schools, largely middle class) and schools with relatively high proportions of such students (Type II schools, largely lower class). They found that, in general, greater openness was more conducive to independence and favorable attitudes toward school, teacher, and self. But student achievement was unassociated with program openness in Type I schools and negatively associated with openness in Type II schools.

Next, we can turn to Wright (1975), who compared 100 fifth-grade children — 50 enrolled in a traditional and 50 enrolled in an open school. The pupils were "balanced" as to socioeconomic status, ability, and previous achievement. After two and one-half years, the pupils in the traditional, or formal, school were found to have achieved higher scores in all nine areas of the Stanford Achievement Test. Further, pupils in the formal school had lower levels of school anxiety. Yet the two groups of pupils did not differ significantly in cognitive style, feelings of control over their own success, self-esteem, or creativity. Wright concluded that "the children of the open school have a conspicuous deficiency in the academic skill areas" (p. 460). As Friedlander (1975) noted in his remarks on Wright's study:

> The open classroom advocates must now recognize that the burden is increasingly upon them to accommodate their enthusiasm to these data, and that they must find improved ways to substantiate the values their vision proposes to advance (p. 468).

A similar study was reported at about the same time by Ward and Barcher (1975). They also compared children who had been matched — on age, grade, IQ, sex, and socioeconomic status. Of 98 pupils, half had been taught in traditional and half in open second-, third-, and fourth-grade classes. The high-IQ children taught in traditional classes were found to be substantially superior to those taught in open classes in both reading and figural (nonverbal) creativity scores.

From Ward and Barcher, we can turn to Röhr (1976), who compared third- and sixth-grade students in open and traditional schools in Malmö, Sweden. This investigator concluded that

> In grade 6 students in the low and intermediate groups at ordinary schools have succeeded somewhat better than corresponding student groups in the open-plan schools. The high group students have similar results at both types of school. In grade 3 the relation between the type of school and the results in the standardized tests is less clear-cut. Here too there is a tendency for the results to be slightly better at the ordinary schools (p. 12).

A study in Winnipeg (Bell, Zipursky, & Switzer, 1976) compared 57 beginners in an informal, or open-area, program and 112 in traditional, formal classrooms. Pretests showed the children to be highly similar in average age, IQ, socioeconomic status, and a variety of perceptual, cognitive, and motor skills. Yet the children in the traditional programs were considerably superior in reading and vocabulary at the end of each of the subsequent three years of schooling, and by the end of the third year they were also superior in mathematical computation. Although two matched groups of fourth graders differed in several mean scores on a personality inventory, the scores remained within "normal limits." The authors noted that "the children not under close supervision in a small group in the informal classroom wasted much of their time in aimless wandering about, in watching movements of other classes, and interacting without useful purpose with their own classmates" (p. 241).

A large-scale study of the relationship of "innovativeness" to achievement was made by the American Institutes for Research (1976). Innovativeness was defined as including

Individualization in Decision Making,
Individualization of Instructional Pace,
Use of Performance Agreements,
Utilization of Student Evaluation [for evaluating student needs and
    modifying a student's instructional program],
Utilization of Objectives,
Teacher or Locally Developed Materials,
Scheduling Characteristics,
Classroom Group Organization,
Teaching Unit Composition, and
Completeness of Instructional Package (pp. 9–10).

The measure of the degree of individualization was based on the first four of these dimensions. All dimensions were measured with a guide used by trained school visitors to describe the basic educational attributes of the school programs, using data from interviews with principals and teachers, classroom observations, and existing school documentation. The guide was used to form groups of students undergoing the same educational experience.

It seems appropriate to regard innovation and individualization as defined in this extensive survey as having much in common with open and informal kinds of teaching. If so, it becomes noteworthy here that "the impact of Level of Innovation was *negative* — that is, the greatest educational growth [in reading and arithmetic achievement during the third grade] occurred in programs with a more moderate emphasis on innovation; . . . [furthermore,] the consistent overachievers actually tended to be members of programs with a lower Level of Innovation or Degree of Individualization" (p. 14).

Finally, we consider a widely noted comparison of formal and informal teaching in England, in a study by Neville Bennett, with Joyce Jordan, George Long, and Barbara Wade (1976). As Jerome Bruner (1976) summarized the findings in his foreword to Bennett's book,

> The more formal the teaching, the more time the pupils spend working on the subject matter at hand. [The subject matter included English, mathematics, and reading.] And in general, . . . the more time pupils spend working on a subject, the more they improve at it — not a huge surprise, but one that grows in importance as one looks at the other results . . . pupils in informal settings did *not* do any better on their creative writing (p. ix).

This study was described in the *New York Times* (May 8, 1976) and the *Saturday Review* (March 19, 1977). As is true of most research thus widely noted, the Bennett study has been much criticized. The criticisms are worth mentioning here because they call attention to some of the pitfalls of this kind of research. Thus, Good (1977) pointed out that no measures of pupil aptitude were used as controls and that the observations of pupils were unaccompanied by observations of the teachers.

Similarly, J.L. Powell (1976) questioned the validity of Bennett's classifying teachers into three categories (formal, mixed, and informal) in that such terms "relate only to some broad tendencies observable in the teaching of some teachers" (p. 1). This inadequate detail arose from the lack of observation of the teachers and the reliance on a teacher questionnaire whose questions were, according to Powell, unclear and ambiguous. The validation of the questionnaire responses through observation of a sample of teachers was itself inadequate. Then the method of clustering the teachers permitted much possibly important variation within clusters. This variation was even more apparent within the broader types (formal, mixed, and informal), which shared characteristics with one or both of the other groups. Moreover, it was erroneous to use the pupil instead of the class as the unit of analysis; if the class had been used, the results would have been "much less likely" to be statistically significant. (But, we should note, the direction and amount of the difference would probably not change greatly if the class were used as the unit of analysis.) Further, the social class of the pupils was unknown and uncontrolled.

In their critique of Bennett's study, Rogers and Baron (1977) pointed out, first, the inconsistency between Bennett's claim that the teachers were chosen by a random procedure and the fact that the teachers *agreed* to participate. Second, Bennett had noted many uncontrolled differences between the formal and informal classrooms: for instance, the traditional, or formal, teachers tended more often than the more informal teachers to be older, more experienced, married, and teaching more often in Roman Catholic schools, in nonrural schools, and in schools with fewer immigrant children. Third, Bennett extrapolated from norms in the manual of the Edinburgh Reading Test in a possibly unwarranted way in obtaining scores for brighter older children but failed to use this extrapolation for low-achieving boys in informal classrooms where the technique might have favored the informal classrooms. Fourth, 5 of the 12 formal, but only 3 of the 13 informal, classes took the highly motivating 11-plus examination during the school year. Fifth, the differences between groups, in view of the differences within groups, are of little or no educational importance.

After an extensive compilation of these criticisms, along with some of their own, Gray and Satterly (1976) concluded that "no valid conclusions can be reached in terms of the published evidence" (p. 46). Yet it seems unjustified to draw no plausible and probable inferences from Bennett's study, along the lines of Bennett's own conclusions.* Although the critics do offer rival hypotheses to explain Bennett's findings, their alternatives themselves remain unproven.

These criticisms of Bennett's study illustrate the point, made earlier, that educational research is likely to be flawed. Seldom does a researcher in the behavioral sciences anticipate all possible criticisms. And the exigencies of the real world may in any case vitiate his research.

Thus the path to increasing certainty becomes not the single excellent study, which is nonetheless weak in one or more respects, but the convergence of findings from many studies, which are also weak but in many different ways. The dissimilar, or nonreplicated, weaknesses leave the replicated finding more secure. Where the studies do not overlap in their flaws but do overlap in their implications, the research synthesizer can begin to build confidence in those implications.

Studies in Variables of Teaching

More evidence is available. It takes the form of many studies of specific variables in teacher behavior in relation to pupil achievement in reading and mathematics in the early grades. Those studies have been reviewed, sifted, analyzed, and collated by several writers, for example, Barak Rosenshine (1976), Donald Medley (1977), and by John Crawford, Nicholas Stayrook, and me (Program on Teaching Effectiveness, CERAS, 1977).

Methods of reviewing and synthesizing research differ as much as methods of doing research. Rosenshine considered all the findings he could

---

*Acceptance of Bennett's findings is supported in B. Rosenshine's review (*American Education Research Journal*, 1978, *15*, 163-169).

TABLE 2

Information Concerning Variables to be Considered
in Developing a Teacher Education Program

Name of Variable and Study in which Investigated	Operational Definition with References and Page Numbers
G2.1 Teacher reactions to wrong answers: criticism (BE, 1974, var. 29, p. 118).	"Responses coded as *incorrect answers* are those in which the child's response is treated as simply wrong by the teacher. The teacher need not explicitly tell the child that he is wrong; he may indicate this indirectly by searching for the answer from someone else or by providing it himself" (BE, 1973, Appendix A, p. 13). "Criticism . . . refers to negative teacher evaluative reactions that go beyond the level of simple negation by expressing anger or personal criticism of the child in addition to indicating the incorrectness of his response . . . Any verbal response which disparagingly refers to the child's intellectual ability or, more frequently, his motivation to do good work, is coded as criticism" (BE, 1973, Appendix A, p. 16).

SOURCE: Program on Teaching Effectiveness, CERAS (1977, p. A-94).
NOTE: BE=Brophy & Evertson.

r with Adjusted Reading Achievement	Mean	S.D.	Metric and Interpretation
$r = .61$ in year two, high SES, reading group context (BE, 1974, var. 29, p. 118)	2% (unpublished computer table)	7%	The metric for this variable is the percentage of incorrect answers which were followed by teacher verbal criticism. ". . . the data for teacher criticism of the student's answer revealed generally positive correlations, and all those which reached statistical significance were positive. Note that all of the latter [statistically significant +r's] are for high SES schools only" (BE, 1974, p. 43). ". . . the most successful teachers in high SES schools tended to be demanding and somewhat critical when student performance failed to measure up to expectation" (BE, 1974, p. 44). Teachers of high SES pupils should use verbal criticism sparingly (criticizing about 1 out of 10 incorrect responses), but sufficiently, to communicate high expectation to students.

track down and based his interpretations on the consistency of their direction. Medley paid attention only to correlation coefficients that equalled at least .39 and were statistically significant at the .05 level. My coworkers and I focused entirely on four major, relatively large-scale correlational studies of teaching. These were studies by Jere Brophy and Carolyn Evertson (1974), Frederick McDonald and Patricia Elias (1976), Robert Soar (1973), and Jane Stallings and David Kaskowitz (1974). We analyzed the results of the four studies in detail, looking at their definitions of variables and the correlations of the variables with pupil achievement in reading.

It is especially worth noting that we took into account the averages and variabilities of the measures of teacher behavior. The importance of the average level and the variability, usually disregarded in research reviewing, can be seen in the study by Brophy and Evertson, which dealt with a teacher behavior labeled "Teacher reactions to wrong answers: criticism." As shown in Table 2, this variable correlated .61, that is, positively and strongly, with adjusted pupil achievement in reading in classes of higher socioeconomic status. On the face of it, this correlation implies that teachers would do well to criticize pupils in such classes frequently. But further examination revealed that incorrect responses amounted to only about 20 to 25 percent of all pupil responses. Further, the mean for the measure of all verbal criticism was only about 5 to 10 percent, and its variability (as measured by its standard deviation) was only about 7 percent. If we take about 8 percent of 25 pecent, we obtain about 2 percent of all teacher reactions to pupil responses as the mean frequency of criticism after incorrect pupil responses among these teachers. Thus the high correlation means that the more effective teachers gave criticism only a very small percentage of the time, and only with pupils of higher socioeconomic status, while the less effective teachers *never* gave such criticism.

In any event, we carefully sifted in this way the detailed information for several hundred variables in teacher behavior and classroom activity. From this sifting we developed a set of inferences as to how third-grade teachers should work if they wish to maximize achievement in reading and, we think, also in mathematics, for children either higher or lower in academic orientation.

Inferences from Studies of Variables

What are these inferences? I present only a few of them here, in the form of summary "teacher-should" statements, without the specifics that accompany them. They must be qualified implicitly with all the assumptions as to objectives and context that I have already mentioned. In their full form, they take a fairly "low-inference" cast, which means that they refer to ways of teaching that are relatively specific and objectively observable and that require relatively little extrapolation from terminology to what is to be done. Further, these "teacher-should" statements seem consistent with the conclusions of Rosenshine, Medley, and others.

Here they are:

— Teachers should have a system of rules that allow pupils to attend to their personal and procedural needs *without* having to check with the teacher.

— Teachers should move around the room a lot, monitoring pupils' seatwork *and* communicating to their pupils an awareness of their behavior, while also attending to their academic needs.

— When pupils work independently, teachers should insure that the assignments are interesting and worthwhile yet still easy enough to be completed by each third grader working without teacher direction.

— Teachers should keep to a minimum such activities as giving directions and organizing the class for instruction. Teachers can do this by writing the daily schedule on the board, insuring that pupils know where to go, what to do, etc.

— In selecting pupils to respond to questions, teachers should call on a child by name *before* asking the question as a means of insuring that all pupils are given an equal number of opportunities to answer questions.

— With *less* academically oriented pupils, teachers should always aim at getting the child to give some kind of response to a question. Rephrasing, giving cues, or asking a new question can be useful techniques for bringing forth some answer from a previously silent pupil or one who says "I don't know" or answers incorrectly.

— During reading-group instruction, teachers should give a maximal amount of brief feedback and provide fast-paced activities of the "drill" type.

One way to sum up many of the implications of the research, as embodied in these "teacher-should" statements, is to say that teachers should organize and manage their third-grade classes so as to optimize what Berliner and his coworkers (1976) call "academic learning time" — time during which pupils are actively and productively engaged in their academic learning tasks. And one way to do this is to avoid time-wasting activities, for example, waiting in line to have papers corrected or receive further instructions. Note here the consistency of these statements with the conclusions from comparisons of direct and open patterns of teaching.

Whatever impression this sample of inferred recommendations may make, one aspect should be clear: they are not unnecessary in the sense that all or almost all teachers are already behaving in these ways. These ways of behaving would not have survived the research process if they did not correlate positively with pupil achievement. And they could not have correlated positively with pupil achievement unless there had been substantial variability among teachers in the degree to which they behaved in these ways.

The teaching implied by these recommendations may seem excessively task-oriented, with no room for exploration, creativity, and self-direction. But this need not be the case. The children's success in their well-organized tasks can make them happy with school and themselves. Also, Rosenshine has seen classes in which mornings were devoted to the business of acquiring skill in reading and mathematics, and afternoons were given over to games, free exploration, and creative work. If such classes are effective, what I have described would apply only to the mornings, and what open school adherents advocate would apply to the afternoons. But it should not be forgotten that what I have described has emerged from research. It is the joint yield, the convergence, the common general finding of years of careful classroom observation, reliable and valid measurement, and sophisticated statistical work.

The Need for Experimentation

Note that very few of the studies I have cited in building the case for a scientific basis of the art of teaching meet the requirement of having satisfactorily demonstrated causal effects. As correlational studies, they must inevitably be weak in this respect, and subject to the same kind of endless argument that goes on about whether cigarette smoking actually causes lung cancer. The dispute between the American Tobacco Institute and the National Cancer Institute still has a logical and theoretical basis, even though the converging correlational evidence of many kinds has long since settled the matter for most of us. Only an ethically impossible experiment would end the doubt in terms of the logic of scientific method. In that experiment, one group of humans randomly assigned would be subjected to decades of cigarette smoking while the remaining members of the group being experimented with would refrain from smoking.

The same is true in teaching; we shall not know whether the direct, structured, formal approaches actually cause higher achievement than progressive, open, and informal methods until true experiments can be performed. Fortunately, unlike the cigarette-smoking experiment, such an enterprise on teaching is ethically and otherwise feasible, as I shall demonstrate in Chapter II.

The Alternative to Scientific Method

What are the alternatives to the effort to build a scientific basis for the art of teaching? For most of our history, the main alternative has been a combination of logic, clinical insight, raw experience, common sense, and the writings of persuasive prose stylists. One such influential piece of writing — one that greatly spurred the open education movement in this country — was recently described by Goodlad (1977) as "merely one man's intuitive observation of an unidentified sample of schools. [The author] left no instruments, no specification of sample, no trail for others to follow"(p. 3).

Since *Summerhill* appeared in 1960, we seem to have been more than ever at the mercy of powerful and passionate writers who shift educational thinking ever more erratically with their manifestos. The kind of research I have been describing is a plodding enterprise, the reports of which are seldom, I regret to say, as well written as the pronouncements of authors unburdened by scientific method. But, in the long run, the improvement of teaching — which is tantamount to the improvement of our children's lives — will come in large part from the continued search for a scientific basis for the art of teaching.

CHAPTER II

Applying What We Know: The Field of Teacher Education

I N CONSIDERING how a scientific basis for the art of teaching can be applied, we obviously become concerned with teacher education. It is in that field that the application takes place — in preservice teacher education, where prospective teachers are prepared, and in inservice teacher education, where teachers already on the job improve their ability to do the job.

The importance of teacher education is commensurate with the importance of teaching itself. We do not want our children to be influenced by persons to whom we have failed to give the best possible preparation for their task. Nor do we want our enormous investment in teaching to yield anything but the best possible returns for our society.

THE STATE OF TEACHER EDUCATION

As everyone knows, teacher education has a long history of low status. It is possible to find statements concerning its poor condition in the nineteenth century and all through the twentieth. In our own time, that undesirable state of affairs has been set forth in volumes by James Bryant Conant (1963) and James Koerner (1963), and in *Teacher Education,* a yearbook of the National Society for the Study of Education edited by Kevin Ryan (1975).

Many of the criticisms of teacher education deal with its governance and only incidentally with its content. The debates on content are concerned with relative emphasis on liberal education and subject matter competence as against more strictly "education" courses, such as those in curriculum and teaching methods. The problem of content is seen in turn to be involved with governance — the distribution of power over teacher education. Liberal arts faculties, education faculties, organizations of teachers and administrators, and state education departments engage in struggles for this power. Such struggles were expressed in the 1950s in the writings of Arthur Bestor and Harold Hand.

Yet in a recent series of articles (Messerli, 1977; Wallace, 1977; LoPresti, 1977; Spencer & Boyd, 1977; King, Hayes, & Newman, 1977) it was repeatedly recognized that the power struggle is not more important than the research struggle for knowledge about teaching. Who determines what teachers should learn does not matter so much as what kinds of knowledge and what skills in teaching have been identified as worth learning. In short, although no armistice between the warring camps should be expected, the competition for control of teacher education should take second place to our concern with establishing a scientific basis for the art of teaching.

Thus, the poor state of teacher education is attributable, in part at least, to an insufficiency of the kind of scientific basis I have tried to sketch. This kind of explanation can be seen in the history of medical education. That field was diagnosed by Abraham Flexner (1910), in his epochal *Medical Education in the United States,* as extremely sick. He was able to bring about a cure, however, because even in his time medicine was "part and parcel of modern science." The scientific basis for the art of medical practice was imperfect in 1910 — even more so, of course, than it is today. In Flexner's words, medical science dealt "not only with certainties but also with probabilities, surmises, theories." Yet, because medicine had a scientific basis, the weakness of medical education in 1910 could be contrasted with the strength of the scientific knowledge that medical research had built. We all know that the Flexner Report was able to raise medical education to a wholly new level because of the strength of that profession's scientific basis.

Clifford (1973) has documented in detail the forlorn "history of the impact of research on teaching." That history is a record of premature hopes dashed upon the realities of inadequate scientific bases. Educational innovations can indeed spread and become widely adopted — often to an extent and with a rapidity unjustified by the scientific basis for the innovation. The Roman-candle history of teaching machines (Markle, 1976) provides just one example. But more solidly established bases for change in teacher education — in the application of scientific knowledge about teaching — can lead to a happier history. Teacher education should rise to a wholly new level as the scientific basis of the art of teaching becomes stronger.

KNOWLEDGE THAT VS. KNOWLEDGE HOW

It is important at the outset to make clear the need for knowledge of a new kind of relationship if teacher education is to apply what we have by way of a scientific basis for the art of teaching. This new relationship is one between teacher education policies, procedures, and techniques, on the one hand, and teaching methods and styles, on the other. Until now we have been concerned with teacher behavior — in all its ramifications, including teacher–pupil interaction and the creation of classroom environments — as the independent variable. But when we come to teacher education, we must look upon teacher behavior as the dependent variable.

Further, we are not so much concerned here with the teacher's "knowing that" as with his or her "knowing how." This distinction, made by the analytic philosopher Gilbert Ryle (1949), refers to the difference between being able to state factual propositions and being able to perform skills or operations. The one kind of knowledge does not necessarily follow from the other. For example, we may know *that* reinforcers strengthen responses but not know *how* to reinforce a pupil so as to strengthen the child's tendency to participate in class discussions. Similarly, we may know *that* criticism in very small amounts may be good for the achievement of more academically oriented pupils but not know *how* to limit our criticism to those small amounts for that kind of pupil.

Much of the teacher education program is given over to providing teachers with a great deal of knowledge *that* certain things are true: in the subjects to be taught; in the historical, philosophical, social, and psychological foundations of education; in the curriculum and instruction of various subject matter fields; and so on. This kind of knowledge is acquired by prospective teachers in the courses taught by teacher education faculties, with all the paraphernalia and methods used in college teaching in general. For the most part, this aspect of teacher education has proceeded along much the same lines as those that have been followed in courses in the sciences and humanities — in English, history, philosophy, chemistry, or mathematics — at the college level.

In recent years, however, an additional approach toward helping teachers know and understand concepts has been used. This is the "protocol materials" approach. It consists of developing films or videotapes to be viewed by the teacher. The materials show instances, occurring in real or almost real settings, of particular categories of teacher behavior (e.g., approving or probing). After viewing the materials, the teacher should be able to recognize instances of a particular category and to categorize occurrences in real classrooms appropriately.

In one program for developing protocol materials, Gliessman and Pugh (1976) produced films showing instances of the concepts of *approving, disapproving, probing, informing, reproductive (lower-order) questioning,* and *productive (higher-order) questioning.* Shown to students in educational psychology courses, the films raised scores on tests of ability to categorize these behaviors and received favorable ratings from the instructors and their students. It seems clear that protocol materials can go a long way toward reducing the hitherto almost total reliance on words as the medium by which teachers are helped to understand the concepts and phenomena entailed in their work.

Practice

When it comes to providing prospective or already employed teachers with knowledge *how,* we know that practice is required — as another analytic philosopher, Jane Roland (1961), has pointed out. "Jones could not know how to swim or speak French unless he had at some time practiced swimming or tried to speak French" (p. 61). It is this realization of the need for practice that has led from the very beginning to the inclusion in teacher education programs of opportunities for practice teaching.

Yet common sense and research results agree in finding that practice alone is not enough. If it were, teachers would automatically improve in performance as they gained more years on the job. But the fact is that at least nine studies have shown only a very low correlation, if any, between years of teaching experience and the average achievement of the teacher's students (Rosenshine, 1971, pp. 201–205).

Those studies were made with teachers already in service. What about the practice of budding teachers? Here the practice is accompanied by the observation, guidance, and advice of the regular classroom teacher, who provides a model as well — one from which the student teacher can presumably learn.

Student Teaching and Beyond

Student teaching has been the subject of much thinking, writing, and even some research over the decades. In general, it has been considered to be the single best, though far from faultless, component of teacher education programs. It has often been indicted as too unsystematic or unplanned, as unmanageable in its complexity, and as too much at the mercy of the idiosyncrasies of the cooperating and supervising teachers. Some appraisals have shown that student teachers hardly change their ways of teaching at all, from the beginning to the end of the student teaching period — and even that their attitudes and behavior tend to deteriorate, at least in the view of those who value nonauthoritarianism and nonpunitiveness in teaching.

It has been demonstrated that skill in simple and complex motor tasks continues to improve over hundreds and even thousands of trials (Hudgins, 1974). Apparently, knowledge of results continues to operate to improve motor skills even over protracted practice. In student teaching, however, such feedback or knowledge of results seldom comes through clearly or quickly enough to improve performance. The feedback may be delayed for days or weeks, or never appear at all.

Hudgins (1974) has derived from research on the learning of complex skills certain principles that should apply to the acquisition and use of teaching skills, such as the teaching of concepts (Clark, 1971). In teaching concepts, the teachers should first assess the pupil's preinstructional knowledge. Second, the teacher should define the concept and offer clear, positive instances along with indications of their critical characteristics. Third, the teacher should gradually mix negative instances into the examples, asking the student to indicate whether each does or does not meet the criteria of the concept, and give the student feedback after each response. Finally, the teacher should evaluate the student's learning of the concept.

To prepare teachers to carry out such steps, teacher education should provide for the teacher's (a) learning the general model of the teaching skill; (b) practicing the skill in a self-contained setting, one that is easily arranged and does not require students and supervisors but does provide the teacher with feedback; and (c) practicing the skill in the actual classroom. Using this conception of teacher preparation led Hudgins to a restatement of the already well-established concept of self-contained materials for teacher education — a concept we shall consider in various forms. Here we note only that this concept represents a major effort to overcome the limitations of the student teaching arrangement that was for too long the sole vehicle of practice for prospective teachers.

TECHNIQUES FOR CHANGING TEACHER BEHAVIOR

Thus we see that the limitations of student teaching made teacher education receptive when alternatives began to be offered. The time for more varied and manageable approaches had come.

Microteaching

In the 1960s, teacher educators fell hungrily upon the innovation called microteaching. Microteaching caught on rapidly. Within a few years it was being used, in one form or another, in 176 programs for educating secondary school teachers in the United States (B. E. Ward, 1970). I am also aware of its being used in several other countries, including Australia, Canada, England, West Germany, Israel, Nigeria, and Sweden.

As is well known, microteaching is scaled-down teaching — teaching conducted for only five or ten minutes at a time, with only five or ten students, and focused on only one or a few aspects of the teacher's role. The teacher tries, say, reinforcing participation or making an assignment, rather than undertaking the whole of what a teacher does, in all its multifaceted complexity, with a class of 30 for a whole period of instruction.

The advantages of microteaching become evident as soon as one encounters this intriguing idea. Such an arrangement is at the least more manageable and controllable. It does not take up whole hours and classes in order to give the neophyte an introduction to teaching. It does not induce the anxiety that accompanies facing a whole class for a whole period. It allows concentration on one part of teaching at a time — just as the violinist can play the same few bars again and again.

Not only was microteaching widely adopted; it was closely studied. The technique lends itself to easy variation and manipulation, and many of the possibilities were quickly tried. For example, the value of providing the microteaching teacher with a model was investigated, and different kinds of models — live, videotaped, or merely printed — were compared to determine their effectiveness in promoting the teacher's acquisition of a given skill. Also, the feasibility of teaching peers rather than actual pupils was investigated. The number of pupils taught was varied. The kinds of supervision and feedback provided the teacher were studied, particularly as to the value of videotaped feedback. And the interval between the first and second microteaching sessions was permitted to range from a few minutes to a week.

The results of many of these investigations have been reviewed by Turney, Clift, Dunkin, and Traill (1973), writing in Australia. I mention this work only to indicate the enthusiasm and industry that greeted this first major departure from the traditional sole reliance on student teaching as the vehicle by which the prospective teacher could get some practice. For our purposes, let it suffice to say that microteaching has generally been found to be effective in the sense that teachers do exhibit the kinds of behavior at which the microteaching is aimed — not only in the hours or days immediately following the microteaching but in the subsequent months and at the end of the first year of actual teaching as well (Trinchero, 1975). Compared with traditional observation and teaching experience, microteaching produced teachers judged to have higher degrees of competence and more favorable attitudes toward their teacher education programs.

Nonetheless, microteaching research has not yielded many firm conclusions concerning the value of the many variations possible within this approach to teacher practice. It may be that such research has erred in regarding the technique too much as a vehicle for increasing *knowledge how* and too little as a means for influencing *knowledge that*. Such a conclusion seems to follow from the studies conducted and reviewed by MacLeod and McIntyre (1977). Their work led them to a new rationale for microteaching as a teacher education technique — a rationale that emphasizes teachers' cognitions. Microteaching can thus be regarded as primarily a way of influencing cognitive structures that are important in teaching. Such structures, they held, should give teachers conceptually simple guides by which to govern their behavior in the hundreds of interpersonal interactions occurring in a day's classroom work.

Minicourses

Microteaching was developed primarily for use in preservice teacher education. It was relatively unwieldy in inservice teacher education, where supervisors and videotape recording machine operators were usually hard to come by. What was needed was a relatively self-administrable version of the microteaching idea. This was soon forthcoming in the form of Minicourses

(Borg, Kelley, Langer, & Gall, 1970). Minicourses are packages of materials, including manuals, self-administered tests, and films, intended for use with videotape or audiotape recorders in rooms and with pupils furnished by the school.

With one typical Minicourse the teacher can acquire training in "Organizing Independent Learning: Primary Level." First, the teacher reads about a set of skills in the teacher's handbook; second, she views a film explaining and illustrating those skills; third, she plans and teaches a lesson in which she practices the skills; and fourth, she evaluates her lesson. The practice is performed both in a microteaching format, with only three or four pupils outside the regular classroom, and in the regular classroom with the entire class. This Minicourse takes about an hour a day for 16 days over about a four-week period. In general, the course is aimed at helping teachers to establish with pupils the concept of working independently, to give pupils facility in solving problems that arise during independent work periods, to develop appropriate expectations about the promptness or delay of teacher response to pupil work, and finally to combine independent work, problem solving, and delayed response into a learning environment that facilitates independent activity and small-group instruction.

All in all, about a dozen Minicourses have been developed, tested, and marketed. The testing consists of an experiment in which teachers are first observed to determine the preexisting level of the teaching skills at which the Minicourse is aimed. Then the Minicourse is individually self-administered by the teachers. The teachers are observed again by trained observers who determine the quality of the behaviors in the teacher's actual classroom some time after the end of the Minicourse.

Borg (1972) carried out what may be the most convincing demonstration of Minicourse effectiveness thus far. Among the behaviors influenced were "Redirecting the same question to several pupils," "Framing questions that call for longer pupil responses," "Seeking further clarification and pupil insight," and "Not repeating pupil answers." He made videotape recordings of each of 24 teachers before, immediately after, 4 months after, and 39 months after training. Analyses of the recordings showed that the Minicourse significantly changed most of the 10 question-asking behaviors that the Minicourse was intended to influence. Borg concluded that "after 39 months, the performance of the subjects was still significantly superior to their precourse performance on 8 of the 10 behaviors that were scored" (p. 572). It might be objected that the teachers knew their behaviors were being recorded and hence behaved as they had been influenced to behave only to please the investigator. But this possibility seems remote simply because the behaviors cannot be turned on and off that easily. It seems improbable that teachers could exhibit these 10 behaviors unless the behaviors had become fairly well established in the teacher's normal practice.

Other Methods of Changing Teacher Behavior

With microteaching and Minicourses, teacher educators acquired tools that seemed to have demonstrable effectiveness in improving the teacher's "knowledge how." These approaches received the widest attention and were subjected to the most research. But they were not the only procedures that appeared on the teacher education scene during the sixties and seventies. For example, Flanders (1970) had accumulated much evidence about teachers who learned and used his interaction analysis categories to observe and analyze their own behavior or who received information about their behavior in terms of these categories. Such teachers usually made some successful attempt to change their behavior to make it accord more closely with their own previously unarticulated conceptions of desirable teaching.

Similarly, Wagner (1973) compared the effectiveness of microteaching and cognitive discrimination training in bringing about student-centered teaching on the part of undergraduates (prospective teachers). The discrimination training consisted of presenting the undergraduates, four at a time, with 33 recorded teacher replies to student comments. The prospective teachers had been supplied with a brief description of six subcategories of teacher replies (namely, "asking for clarification," "restating," and "using students' ideas" — all considered to be parts of *student*-centered teaching — and "asking a directive question," "arguing," and "ignoring" — all considered to be aspects of *teacher*-centered teaching). The undergraduates coded the taped teacher responses one at a time and then, after each coding, were told the correct answer and given a short explanation. The training lasted about 30 minutes. Another group of undergraduates engaged in microteaching for about 30 minutes. Subsequently, both groups of undergraduates prepared and taught a new lesson. It turned out that the discrimination training was significantly more effective than the microteaching in bringing about student-centered teaching. Thus, learning to discriminate was sufficient to bring about behavioral change. In this instance, and perhaps in many others, the more elaborate microteaching procedure could be replaced by this less expensive kind of training.

Another demonstration of the possibility that simple techniques can change teacher behavior was provided by Good and Brophy (1974). They used a single interview to provide a teacher with feedback based on observations of the teacher — feedback intended to help change teacher behavior toward selected students. Each teacher was at once informed and advised about his or her own behavior toward various pupils. Thus

> in making suggestions for improvement the authors were in effect saying, "You are doing a fine job with Mary; now try to do the same kinds of things with Jane." This is much less threatening and more acceptable than "your way is wrong, do it my way" (p. 291).

Using this approach, Good and Brophy identified pupils who participated much less than the average and also pupils who seldom were encouraged by the teacher to make a second or an extended response to a question. The teachers were given the names of these pupils as well as the names of pupils whom the teachers *were* treating appropriately. As a result of the interview, the teachers agreed to seek responses more persistently from the appropriate pupils and also, although less readily, to call more frequently on pupils who were infrequent participants and to initiate more private interactions with them. Subsequent observations in each classroom showed that the teachers had changed substantially in the directions intended.

There is another way to change teacher behavior that is even less expensive than the discrimination training provided by Wagner or the interviews conducted by Good and Brophy. The technique has been used, especially at the college level, and found to be moderately effective. It consists of using students' descriptions of their teachers on rating scales as feedback to the teachers. Such feedback has been used with sixth-grade teachers given their pupils' ratings (Gage, Runkel, & Chatterjee, 1963), with elementary school principals given their teachers' ratings (Daw & Gage, 1967; Burns, 1977), and with social studies department chairmen given the department members' ratings (Hovenier, 1966).

Discrepancy influences the technique's effectiveness. Thus, Centra (1973) showed that the feedback to teachers of college students' ratings produced change in the teachers' behavior only when there were marked discrepancies between the teacher's self-rating, or self-perception, and the students' ratings. Similarly, the greater the discrepancy between teacher's ratings of their ideal and their actual department chairman, the greater the change in the department chairman's behavior as a consequence of the feedback, as compared with the change in a group that did not receive the feedback (Hovenier, 1966).

Such ratings are altogether inexpensive. The technique requires no interviews or observations by professional staff whose salaries must be paid. Thus the feedback of students' ratings can be regarded as a feasible approach to teacher change — but only under certain conditions. For one thing, the pupils must be mature enough to make usable and reliable ratings; the fifth or sixth grade is probably the lower limit in this sense. Second, the teachers must be motivated to change by virtue of their respect for student opinion. Third, as McKeachie (1976) has pointed out, teachers are more likely to change if they receive initial ratings that are moderate rather than extremely high or extremely low. McKeachie considers this finding to be consistent with achievement motivation theory — theory that predicts greater success or change when expectations are neither too high to be realistic nor too low to instigate action. Finally, the feedback may be expected to have an effect only when the teacher has the indicated changes in behavior within his or her repertoire of behaviors — in other words, when the teachers *can* change in the desired direction if they want to. Here, the microteaching and Minicourse techniques could be useful in equipping teachers with desired ways of behaving that they do not already possess.

One last approach seems worth mentioning if only because it rests on the ever-attractive conception of teaching as a performing art. What Stanislavski did to help his actors realize their roles may help teachers comprehend and enact theirs. Travers and Dillon (1975) have worked on this appealing idea. They summarized Stanislavski's method and then presented scenarios for careful study by future teachers. They intend the study to consist of more than reading — the student should analyze the role characteristics, reread the scenario, put himself into the teacher's shoes, act out and speak the parts, and try to experience the appropriate feelings and ideas. Rather than focusing on the teacher's observable performance, this approach emphasizes "inner behavior." It assumes the correct inner behavior will be reflected in appropriate "outer behavior."

In another part of their treatment, Travers and Dillon seem to contradict themselves by telling teachers that, if they will relax their muscles (outer behavior), they will reduce their feelings of tension and anxiety (inner behavior). Here the outer behavior is assumed to control the inner. Also, the authors offer no research evidence that their techniques work. Nonetheless, if it can be put into forms that can be experimentally tested, the idea of training teachers as if they had much in common with actors seems to be worth trying.

THE FIELD OF TEACHER EDUCATION PRODUCTS

Let us turn now to a more general view of the effort to apply a scientific basis for the art of teaching to teacher education. This view takes in the field of teacher education products. These are materials packaged in a form that makes them transportable and relatively self-administrable for use in changing and, it is hoped, improving teaching in some way. Such products have been developed by the hundreds during the last decade, largely as a result of the emphasis on developmental work by the Federal government's Office of Education and National Institute of Education. That emphasis influenced university research and development centers, regional educational laboratories, and many other organizations and workers to produce curriculum packages and materials to help teachers and administrators. The whole enterprise was an attempt to make readily available and highly usable the ideas and techniques that educational research and development workers had formulated. In the past, these ideas had usually gone unused and neglected by the practitioners to whom they could conceivably be helpful.

The Stanford Catalog

The teacher-training products became so numerous that several catalogs of these materials appeared. Finally, the Program on Teaching Effectiveness (1974) at Stanford, in order to meet its own research and development needs, compiled a master catalog stored on computer tape. That catalog identified and described more than 800 products. A teacher-training product was defined as material intended to equip teachers with skills, or knowledge of how to do certain things, rather than merely knowledge that certain things are true. As we put it in a monograph describing the field,

> teacher training products must require the trainee to be active, in the sense of performing, practicing, or trying out the skills to be acquired. Such a requirement rules out training materials that merely ask the trainee to receive information through reading, listening, or viewing (Program on Teaching Effectiveness, 1974, pp. 3–4).

The Stanford catalog described the hundreds of products in terms of nine dimensions:

1. The product's subject matter specificity. (Did it apply to the teaching of English, mathematics, science, social studies, or school subjects in general?)
2. The target audience. (Was the product intended for preservice trainees, inservice teachers, or both?)
3. The grade-level specificity. (Was the teaching skill pertinent to early childhood education, to the high school level, to something in between, or to all levels?)
4. The so-called target outcome. (Which aspects of teaching — such as planning, presentation, interaction with pupils, attitude toward teaching, or the teacher's self-concept — was the product concerned with?)
5. The target outcomes for students. (Which of various kinds of cognitive and social–emotional outcomes?)
6. The training situation. (What materials were provided with the product and what materials and equipment had to be provided by the user?)
7. The time and number of persons required to administer training with the product. (How many trainees could use the product at one time?)
8. The kind of practice provided. (Was it paper-and-pencil exercises, or classifying incidents in a film, or playing a simulated teaching game, or teaching actual students?)
9. The phase of teaching in which the acquired skills would be used. (Did the training apply to the teacher's work before, during, or after interaction with students?)

The NEA/Far West Laboratory Project

The main purpose of the Stanford catalog was to determine in detail what was already available in order to plan the work of the Stanford Center's Program on Teaching Effectiveness. For this reason the catalog was not readily usable by teachers and teacher educators who were interested in considering the products.

The need for putting the information into a more usable form eventually led to a new project conducted by Robert McClure and Robert Luke of the National Education Association with the support of the National Institute of Education and the collaboration of Beatrice Ward of the Far West Laboratory for Educational Research and Development. In this "Pilot Project on Practitioner Selection, Use and Critique of Inservice Education Projects"

(McClure, 1976), many products were examined by teachers, teacher educators, and other potential users. McClure characterized the products as ranging from simple to complex; as providing either individual or large-group instruction; as ranging from cheap to expensive; as using either a single medium or several media; as ranging from homemade to "slickly professional"; as being subject-centered or process-oriented or both; as being oriented toward all levels from early childhood education to college and adult education; as ranging from those that offered undocumented, simply derived claims for effectiveness to those that had been subjected to rigorous field tests; and as varying between empirically based and theoretically based.

From working with practitioners, McClure and his coworkers gained the impression that most teachers were unaware of the existence of the products. Further, it seemed that the most successful products clearly matched teachers' stated needs in such activities as individualizing instruction, managing classrooms, or teaching reading. These products could be used without an outside resource person, could be used and completed over a period of several weeks, employed methods other than merely presenting reading matter, and were attractively but not expensively packaged. Some persons who knew about the products rejected them on the grounds that they imposed others' views of teaching or were unrelated to a local problem. But others viewed the products as "one resource that can help to solve some persistent problems with inservice education" (McClure, 1976, p. 15). This was the view adopted by the NEA/Far West Laboratory Project.

What do these products consist of? The NEA/Far West project described them in terms readily understandable by teachers. Let us consider products intended to help teachers in motivating students, since that problem received the highest average rating for level of interest in an NEA Assessment of Teacher Inservice Education Needs conducted in 1975. Student motivation is one of four categories into which the NEA/Far West project has grouped the more than 50 products it has described in detail. (The other three categories were individualizing instruction, language arts, and classroom management.)

One product, entitled "Motivation Theory for Teachers," was developed in 1967 by Madeline Hunter. It consists of a film and an optional programmed book aimed at interpreting motivation theory so that it can be useful in the daily decisions of teachers. The film deals with six factors that can influence motivation: anxiety in the form of concern for the task; the interest of the task; the feeling tone of the task; the level of difficulty of the task; knowledge of results; and intrinsic rewards. The describer's critique of the film states that it "is appropriate to the objectives stated at the beginning of the film. The technical quality is good. . . . The content of the film appears to be accurate and socially fair."

A second product in this category is entitled "Individually Guided Motivation." It was developed at the Wisconsin Research and Development Center for Cognitive Learning, under the direction of Herbert Klausmeier. It deals with four motivational procedures to be used with elementary school children: adult–child conferences to encourage independent reading; teacher –child conferences for goal setting; older children tutoring younger children; and small-group conferences to encourage self-directed desirable social behavior. The product consists of a textbook to be studied and five films to be viewed and discussed by the teachers. It requires five two-hour sessions or a two-day workshop. Large-group sessions are used to communicate information, show films, and administer self-assessment exercises. Large- or small-group sessions are used to criticize and apply information, discuss practice exercises, and engage in role playing.

This pair of descriptions must suffice to illustrate what is meant by teacher-training products. In general, they have the advantages and disadvantages of textbooks or any other standardized set of instructional materials. The advantage is that they can incorporate more careful thought, planning, and scholarship than most teachers or teacher educators can muster when left to their own resources. Their disadvantage is that they cannot be custom tailored to the needs and capabilities of each teacher who may use them. Thus they run the risk of missing the mark for a particular teacher.

Nevertheless, teacher-training products deserve to be better known and more extensively tried. Toward that end the NEA group, under the direction of Robert Luke, has organized a "Project on Utilization of Inservice Education R & D Outcomes." The project serves teachers and other local users in approximately 80 local education associations and school districts in 16 states across the country. It is intended to assist teachers in identifying problems in teaching the basic skills, to build an information system on training products aimed at improving teaching in the basic skills, to assist in setting criteria for selecting products, and to provide help in adapting the products to local conditions. Descriptions of products are kept in central files at the NEA. An information specialist is available via a toll-free telephone line to help users track down the products that seem most promising. All in all, the system is administratively elaborated and coordinated in such a way that the obstacles of ignorance and information lack should be substantially overcome. Then teacher-training products can be given the fair try they deserve.

TEACHER CENTERS

It should be obvious by now that more is involved in teacher education, both preservice and inservice, than a scientific basis for the art of teaching. We need more than the knowledge and tools that will make teacher education procedures influence teacher behavior and, in turn, make teacher behavior contribute more to student achievement and desirable attitudes. Teacher education products of the kind just described are in themselves only part of what is needed. Beyond them organizational and administrative arrangements are needed to bring together productive combinations of leadership, personnel, time, and money.

One idea for organizing such combinations is the teacher center. As is well known, the idea was born in England (see Thornbury, 1974). It was brought to this country by Americans who saw it there and liked what they saw (Rogers, 1976). In brief, teacher centers are places where teachers can come together with other teachers, and perhaps with other useful persons, such as professors, to do things that will help them teach better.

It would not be appropriate to my topic to attempt a full-scale analysis of the alternative kinds of teacher centers that have been proposed and of the political pulling and hauling that have accompanied their development in this country. These matters have been discussed by Eugenia Kemble (1973) from the point of view of the American Federation of Teachers. She has quoted both the AFT's David Selden and the NEA's David Darland as being opposed to the kind of forced and mandated inservice teacher education that teacher centers would presumably replace. To my mind also, teacher centers should be initiated and controlled by teachers. Other kinds of participants, such as adminstrators, parents, and professors, should come to them only by invitation. Just as practitioners of medicine, law, and engineering take responsibility for their own continuing education, so teachers should have the right to do the job for themselves. This proposition seems to me to follow from any decent respect for the professionalism of teachers.

Teacher-governed teacher centers should learn about teacher education products and procedures as these may commend themselves. Thus these approaches should get a fair chance to prove themselves; and that is all that their developers should ask. In short, these ways of applying knowledge about teaching ought, it seems to me, to stand or fall on their ability to impress teachers favorably and to improve teaching, with only such consultation with research workers and other scholars as teachers may see fit to invite.

Teacher centers that focus on teacher education products have been termed "behaviorally oriented" by Feiman (1977), who also identified two other kinds: the humanistic and the developmental. Both of these involve teachers in less structured activities. The humanistic centers try to help teachers share their own expertise with one another in a secure, supportive, and informal atmosphere; teachers adapt materials on display and talk about how things were made. The developmental centers use advisors and curriculum workshops to get teachers to think about the ways in which they organize their experience and their classrooms and to reexamine their beliefs and teaching behavior.

Each of Feiman's three kinds of centers seems to have advantages. It will be regrettable if the "ideological" differences between the types prevents centers from gaining the advantages of all three types: the structure and focus of behavioral centers using teacher education products; the teacher-centeredness and informality of humanistic centers using unprogrammed encounters; and the conceptual orientation of developmental centers providing advisory services. If I have emphasized teacher education products, it is only because they have most obviously represented ways of applying a scientific basis for the art of teaching. But teacher centers can make those applications in other ways, such as discussion and encounter groups, workshops, advisory services, and the simple process of helping teachers talk to one another.

THE CONNECTIONS BETWEEN TEACHER EDUCATION AND EDUCATIONAL OUTCOMES

Two kinds of causal connections are part of the logic of teacher education. The first kind was considered in Chapter I, where it was argued that something is indeed known about relationships between teaching behaviors and methods, on the one hand, and pupil achievement and attitudes, on the other. The second kind of connection is that between teacher education procedures and teacher behaviors.

Now there ought to be a good connection between the two kinds of connections. That is, (a) teacher education should be aimed at producing (b) the kinds of teacher behaviors that have been shown to be related — preferably causally related — to (*c*) valued kinds of student knowledge, understanding, sensibility, and attitude. Then the $a \longrightarrow b$ connections would contribute to achieving the $b \longrightarrow c$ connections.

The Hiatus between the Two Connections

Strangely enough, the work on each of the two kinds of connections has proceeded almost completely independently of the other. Developers of teacher education procedures have gone ahead with their $a \longrightarrow b$ work without waiting for empirical evidence on $b \longrightarrow c$ connections — evidence that the kinds of teacher behaviors they were trying to bring about were indeed conducive to the achievement of educational goals. There has been too little unification of effort of the kind that would bring research and development on teacher effects, or the effects of different kinds of teacher behavior, into close contact with research and development on ways to bring about those kinds of behavior. In short, the right hand of research on teaching effectiveness has too seldom informed the left hand of research on teacher education of what it has been up to. In other words, we have not had enough $a \longrightarrow b \longrightarrow c$ research.

An example of this kind of divorcement can be seen in the work on teachers' questions. Research has thrown serious doubt on the desirability of so-called higher-order questions — questions that call for thinking and problem-solving rather than mere recall. A fair number of correlational studies and experiments (see especially Rosenshine, 1976, pp. 355–356; Gall, Ward, Berliner, Cahen, Crown, Elashoff, Stanton, & Winne, 1976; Program on Teaching Effectiveness, SCRDT, 1976) have failed to show what many educational thinkers had expected, namely, that teachers who ask more "thought" questions produce pupils with better understanding of the subject matter. Indeed they have more often shown the reverse. Higher proportions of *lower*-order, or recall, questions have usually been accompanied by higher pupil scores on tests of both knowledge and understanding of the subject matter. The research is not yet conclusive on this matter, and more sensitive forms of both the questioning and the achievement variables may eventually yield the results that many writers have led us to expect. Nonetheless, we do not at present have any firm empirical basis for advocating that teachers ask more higher-order questions than they presently ask (a rather low proportion).

The explanation may well be that the give-and-take of the classroom recitation is no place for higher-order questions. Such questions, by definition, require deliberation, which takes time. And pupils feel too harried by social pressures in this setting to benefit from the opportunity to think. This explanation implies that higher-order questions *should* improve understanding when encountered in the course of reading prose, in a setting congenial to quiet deliberation. And this implication is supported by evidence that "higher-order inserted questions are of greater benefit than factual ones" (Faw & Waller, 1976, p. 712).

Notwithstanding this state of affairs with respect to higher-order questions in classroom discussions, teacher education research and development have proceeded to develop techniques, such as Minicourses, for instructing teachers to frame more "questions that require the pupil to use higher cognitive processes" (Borg, 1972). Many other objectives of teacher education have also been adopted and acted upon prior to any demonstration that the particular kinds of behavior were desirable in the sense of fostering achievement and desirable attitudes.

An Illustration of Unified Effort

What is needed is work that unites the effort to show that a certain kind of teacher behavior is desirable with the effort to show that such behavior can be brought about through teacher education. Let me illustrate what is needed by describing an experiment in 33 third-grade classes conducted by the Program on Teaching Effectiveness at Stanford University. Put very briefly, the aim of the experiment was to determine whether teachers instructed to behave in certain ways produce pupils with higher levels of achievement and more desirable attitudes than do teachers who have not received such instruction. The noteworthy feature of the experiment in relation to the point concerning unification of effort is that the teacher education objectives were derived in detail from the results of previous correlational studies. The results of those studies were examined, variable by variable, in terms of (*a*) the exact operational definitions of the teacher behaviors observed, (*b*) the correlations of those behaviors with adjusted measures of pupil achievement in reading, (*c*) the average and the variability across teachers of the frequencies of the given kind of teacher behavior, and (*d*) the implications of the empirical findings for what might be considered desirable in teacher education, given the criterion of pupil achievement in reading (see Table 2, in Chapter I).

This kind of detailed sifting of the evidence concerning hundreds of teacher behavior variables in four recent, relatively large-scale correlational studies provided the basis for the formulation of the "teacher-should" statements presented in Chapter I. That formulation, in turn, was expressed in five sets of reading matter, presented at the rate of one per week to the teachers in the instructed group. The instructed teachers were themselves divided at random into two subgroups. One subgroup received the instruction in a "minimal" form consisting merely of the reading matter and self-scored quizzes on the reading matter. The other subgroup received the instruction in a more traditional, and much more expensive, workshop format. These teachers not only read the material and took the quizzes but they participated in weekly group meetings with an instructional staff. At these meetings, the teachers engaged in role playing, viewed videotape records, and discussed the content and problems considered in the teacher education materials.

This experiment illustrates the kind of linkage between teacher education and teacher effectiveness research that seems to be obviously logical and desirable. Yet only a few examples of it are known. Still fewer of these have developed the linkage with detailed atttention to the correlational findings on teaching effectiveness.

It should also be noted that each of the teachers in both the instructed and the uninstructed groups was observed in detail for 18 full school days during the school year — that is, one day every one to three weeks before, during, and after the teacher education program. And, of course, the pupils and their teachers took batteries of tests of cognitive and noncognitive variables at the beginning and end of the school year.

The broad purposes of the experiment should by now be obvious: It is intended, first, to determine whether teacher behaviors that correlate with pupil achievement have causal efficacy in improving pupil achievement. It will also determine how a cheap and easy way of instructing teachers compares in effectiveness with one that requires a professional and hence expensive teacher education staff.

In summary, to restate the main proposition of this chapter, there are many ways to give teachers knowledge of how to teach. These ways, in all their variety, have been found to work in the sense of getting teachers to behave in ways congruent with the aims of the teacher education effort. Accordingly, the tools needed to apply what we know of a scientific basis for the art of teaching are relatively well in hand. They are being further developed and tested in field programs, such as that of the NEA, and they should receive fair consideration in the teacher centers of the kind being advocated by the AFT. The main need in this field is a closer connection between the work of the teacher education researchers and that of the teacher effectiveness researchers. That closer connection can be seen in efforts to use the findings of correlational studies in experiments whose effects on both teacher behavior and student achievement and attitude are determined.

CHAPTER III

Improving What We Know:
A Reexamination of Paradigms

C AN WE improve what we know as the scientific basis of the art of teaching? To do so is to enhance our knowledge of relationships between what teachers do and what students learn.

The problem of improving such knowledge can be divided into two overlapping component problems. First, there are substantive problems — how to identify more powerful variables to be measured, manipulated, and interrelated. Second, there are methodological problems — how to find better ways of measuring variables and determining their relationships. Finally, we shall take an overall look at the prospect of research on teaching — where it will take us in the years ahead.

Substantive Issues

In discussing ways to improve our variables, we should consider the power of our present variables to explain differences in educational outcomes. That discussion leads us to examine the whole idea of variable analysis, which should not be taken for granted. Then, if we are to continue with variable analysis, we must confront the issue of the proper complexity of variables and take a close look at a recent reexamination of the process–product paradigm in research on teacher effectiveness. Finally, we turn to a newly emphasized kind of variable — the time-on-task variable — and speculate about the kinds of phenomena that should be studied within the time that pupils spend on their learning tasks.

The Power of Variables Investigated Thus Far

Before we take up the question of what variables should be investigated, we should touch upon the efficacy of the variables investigated thus far. This efficacy is often compared with that of preinstructional pupil variables, such as IQ (scholastic aptitude), pretested achievement, and social class background.

In every study of teaching that I know of, such preinstructional pupil variables have accounted for more of the variance in pupil achievement than has either the teacher or the teaching variables. Typically, the pupil's scholastic aptitude or prior achievement, measured before the beginning of instruction, correlates much more highly than do teacher behavior variables with pupil achievement measured at the end of the teaching period. This result appears whether the teaching lasts for fifteen minutes or a whole school year. The correlations of preinstructional variables with postinstructional achievement may be as high as .7 to .9.

Investigators have regarded this fact as a reason for despair about the importance of variables in teaching. Too little variance in achievement remains to be accounted for. It would seem that the total importance of variables in teaching is "inherently trivial" (Heath & Nielson, 1974, p. 481).

Much of this kind of assertion has been misinterpreted as signifying that *teaching* makes little or no difference. Yet the studies have not compared teaching with no teaching. Rather they have compared different kinds of teachers and teaching. And they have concluded essentially that one kind is about as effective as another — in short, that *teaching variables* make little difference.

But it may be that teaching variables have been forced into an unfair comparison. The preinstructional variables against which they have been pitted represent the outcome of years of prior experience and development. During these years, pupil ability and achievement have been influenced not only by genetic variables of much-debated importance. They have also been influenced by dozens of powerful "teachers" in the form of parents, friends, neighborhoods, mass media, and even persons called teachers. So the pupil who arrives at the classroom in September has already been much "taught."

The influences of those years of prior "teaching," by "teachers" who have had more prolonged and intimate opportunities to exert their influence, must be regarded as prior links in a long chain of cause-and-effect relationships. In any model of those causal relationships, the last link represents "pupil achievement." That box becomes the first link representing "pre-instructional variables" in the next round of teacher influence on the pupil. Because the effects are cumulative, each new "teacher" adds to the effects of the preceding "teachers." So the last teacher in the chain cannot be expected to have an effect nearly equal to the total effect of all his or her predecessors. Yet it is that last teacher whose effect is studied in any investigation of the importance of teaching variables. Viewed in this way, the last teacher will inevitably have a seemingly "trivial" effect.

If the variables characterizing the last teacher are trivial, however, are not those descriptive of the next-to-last teacher also trivial? And those of the teacher before that? Such reasoning leads to the conclusion that the pupil achievement we are trying to understand and improve has resulted from a long chain of trivial influences. But pupil achievement, and its variance, is obviously nontrivial — it is the knowledge and understanding on which our civilization rests. Hence, something must be wrong with the methods of analysis that lead us to conclude that teaching variables are trivial. We need alternative kinds of reasoning.

One approach is to develop ways of cumulating the effects of teacher variables over successive teachers. Suppose the differences between teachers of three-year-olds produce 5 percent of the total variance in achievement among their pupils. And the differences between the teachers of four-year-olds produce another, only partially independent, 5 percent. And the differences between kindergarten teachers produce another, only partially independent, 5 percent, and so on, through the school grades. After the pupil has had three teachers, their cumulative effect will account for some percentage greater than 5 percent but less than 15 percent of the total variance in pupil achievement. By the time the pupils' school careers have been completed, the total effects of all their teachers, in terms of the variance in their achievement attributable to differences among their teachers, will have become nontrivial.

The numbers used in this illustration are of the order of magnitude found in present-day studies of teaching. Accordingly, if methods become available for estimating the total importance of teacher variables over all of a pupil's teachers, the importance of teacher variables would be more on a par with preinstructional pupil variables. The behavior of earlier teachers will no longer be deprived of credit for having produced some of the preinstructional pupil variance that now makes the variance attributable to teacher differences look so weak.

In any case, it costs little or nothing for a teacher to behave more often in one way than another. But the effect of that difference in behavior on student achievement, when multiplied by the number of students affected by the teacher over a number of years, can become great.

The Issue of "Variable Analysis"

Because the issue has been raised in a manner that challenges our basic premises, we should examine the whole idea of variables, or so-called variable analysis. Blumer (1969) has questioned the value of variable analysis — that is, of doing research by looking for relationships between variables. He noted the chaotic condition of the selection of variables in sociology, the disconcerting absence of generic variables that stand for abstract categories, and the need for understanding the context of variables in a way not provided by variable analysis. In Blumer's view, the process of interpretation or definition that goes on in human groups and that determines the relationships between independent and dependent variables is at variance with the logical premises of variable analysis.

Therefore Blumer proposes that instead of, or at least in addition to, variable analysis we should study the process of forming a definition of the situation and the factors in that definition that affect behavior. We should devote ourselves to analyzing the operation and formation of human group life as these occur through this process of definition.

In reply, I should point out that the process of definition can itself be analyzed into variables. The intensity, complexity, and veridicality of my definition of a situation — say the situation of giving a lecture — influence the way I lecture. As those variables take on different values, my behavior in the lecture situation can be better understood.

Further, it should be noted that Blumer does not advocate the abandonment of variable analysis but merely a recognition of its inadequacy. What he proposes as a supplement is detailed analysis of process. For our purposes, the process would be what goes on in classrooms. This would be analysis of the kind that many aestheticians, sociologists, linguists, and ethnographers have already initiated in what we shall note below as the "qualitative" approach. Much of this approach, when applied to research on teaching, can be regarded as process description, or the simple noting and describing of instances of various kinds of events or processes. This kind of process description would do much to allay Blumer's concern about the isolation of variable analysis from the operating factors in group life. Sensitive description and analysis of classroom phenomena should lay bare the variables inside the "moving structures" and "supporting context" that characterize the experience and definitions of the persons involved in classroom interaction.

The Complexity of Variables in Studies of Teaching

Thus we must face the problem of the complexity of variables in studies of teaching. When the search for relationships is conducted through correlational studies, the number of variables can be well-nigh unlimited. For example, in the study by Stallings and Kaskowitz (1974), the number of variables referring to teacher behavior, pupil behavior, and classroom environment came to many hundreds. Optical scanners and computers were needed to cope with this detailed description of what went on.

When the search for relationships takes the form of experiments, however, only a much smaller number of independent variables can be handled at a time. In fractional factorial designs, the number of independently manipulable treatments can be considerably increased without inordinately large samples because information about higher-order interactions is sacrificed. Yet even in such designs, the upper limit seems to be about ten to twenty independent variables (Calfee, 1976).

If so, at what level of complexity should the independent variables be set? Any particular level can be criticized on the ground that it could be further analyzed into more specific components. For example, in an experiment conducted at Stanford (Program on Teaching Effectiveness, SCRDT, 1976), we used three independent variables — the teacher's structuring, soliciting, and reacting at either high or low levels. Each of these manipulated variables contained from two to six components. Thus, "high structuring" consisted of:

Reviewing the main idea and facets covered in the lesson
Stating objectives at the beginning of the lesson
Outlining the lesson content
Signaling transitions between parts of a lesson
Indicating important points in a lesson
Summarizing the parts of the lesson as the lesson proceeded
"Low structuring" consisted of the absence of these six teaching behaviors.

It might have been desirable to manipulate these components of structuring independently of one another. The same could have been done for the components of soliciting and reacting. To have done so, however, would have resulted in an unmanageable number of independent variables. The sample size would have had to be much larger than present-day levels of support for research make conceivable. And the problems of training teachers in all or even a fraction of the many possible combinations of that many independent variables would have been insurmountable.

Accordingly, in experimentation at least, risky guesses must inevitably be made concerning the specificity or complexity of the independent variables. The price of excessive specificity is not only the unmanageability of the research but also the likelihood of working with relatively unrealistic or trivial patterns of teacher behavior. It is as if we were to decompose water into hydrogen and oxygen to study the independent effects of water's components; the chemist would properly object that we had destroyed the water in analyzing it. The educator can similarly object that we destroy a teaching method when we take it apart and separately manipulate its components. The price of excessive complexity includes the dangers of combining specific behaviors into internally competing, or self-canceling, clusters and of not knowing what parts of the whole really account for any difference that we find.

Only research experience will yield dependable answers as to the right level of complexity for the independent variables to be manipulated. In early experiments, it seems to me, we should work with relatively complex and supposedly powerful combinations of components. For example, a combination of 22 kinds of teacher behavior into a single treatment was used in a current Stanford experiment in third-grade teaching. Each component of that combination of teacher behaviors had been found through correlational studies by other researchers to be correlated with pupil achievement in reading. If that combination does improve achievement in reading, we can then begin the process of analysis, or peeling away components. That analysis would tell us the relative causal influence of the components of that complex treatment.

Even with the data of the present experiment, it is possible through multivariate regression and path analysis techniques to gain some of the advantage of such analysis. Teacher behavior on each component was observed. Conceivably, the correlations among the components will not be too high, despite their having been manipulated as a single complex in the education program provided for the experimental groups of teachers. In that event, we shall be able to make estimates of the independent contributions of the components to the explanation of variance in pupil achievement and attitude.

Doyle's Critique of the Process–Product Paradigm

Now let us turn to the crucial question of variable selection. Here we gain help from the thoughtful and comprehensive critique of the process–product paradigm recently offered by Doyle (1978). Paradigms are, of course, the overarching approaches and theoretical formulations that determine the major purposes, problems, variables, and methods of research workers.

The Process–Product Paradigm. Without question, the dominant paradigm in research on teaching has been the process–product paradigm, also sometimes called the criterion-of-effectiveness paradigm (Gage, 1963). By this approach, as outlined in Chapter I, we search for "processes" (teacher behaviors and characteristics, in the form of teaching styles, methods, models, or strategies) that predict and preferably cause "products" (that is, educational outcomes in the form of student achievement and attitude).

The process–product paradigm appeals immediately to the instincts of educators. What can be more natural than to seek to improve education through improving the work of the agents of society who come into contact with students? It is through those agents, namely, the teachers, that everything we do about curriculum, school finance, building construction, school administration, school–community relationships, and the rest, comes to the point — the point of making contact with the students through whom society will realize its schools' ideals. It is little wonder that the process–product paradigm has enlisted the allegiance of most of those who have done research on teaching during the past half-century.

This paradigm has not gone unchallenged, however, and Doyle brings some of the challenges before us. Nonetheless, as I shall attempt to show, his criticisms and alternatives have not so much undermined the process–product paradigm as they have strengthened it.

To begin with, Doyle finds the process–product paradigm too narrow. It deals with only two major kinds of variables: teaching behavior variables, or processes, on the one hand, and outcome variables, or products, on the other.

Thus the process–product paradigm omits concern with the events that intervene between teaching behaviors and learning outcomes. Student behaviors in the classroom, antecedent and subsequent class meetings, various kinds of classroom and curriculum resources — all of these tend to be neglected. And even when student behaviors are considered, the process–product paradigm emphasizes the teaching behaviors that brought about these student behaviors. Further, this paradigm makes the arguable assumption that causal influence always flows from teacher to student, even though we know intuitively as well as on the basis of research that students also influence teachers.

Further, the process–product paradigm tends to focus on the frequency of teacher behavior. This results from the preferability of so-called low-inference behaviors, those that can be observed directly, without much interpretation or extrapolation from what is evident to the senses. Thus, we wind up *counting* instances of teacher praise rather than making *judgments* concerning teacher warmth. And we *count* the frequency of vague words rather than *judge* the lack of clarity of the teacher's explanations.

Similarly, we prefer to study teacher behaviors that are stable over time and context, because these are more likely to yield reliable relationships with product variables. Even though such stability is not in itself a token of importance, the emphasis on stability may lead us away from crucial behaviors that do not occur with any high degree of stability, or consistency, from day to day. Thus, according to Doyle, the process–product paradigm leads us to behaviors that seem to be "context proof, teacher-proof, and even student-proof" (p. 169), even though they may not be those that are most important in bringing about learning.

The Mediating-Process Paradigm. As one supplement to the process–product paradigm, Doyle offered what he called the mediating-process paradigm. This refers to an approach that takes into account the student responses and psychological processes that govern learning — such mediating processes as attending, translating, segmenting, rehearsing, task persistence, time utilization, active learning time, and pupil engagement with the learning tasks. Doyle noted that much of the study of mediating processes has been conducted in research on programmed instruction, audiovisual media, and special education. But, he argued, that study has yielded concepts and variables that can enlighten research on classroom teaching. For example, students who visualize connections between two nouns are better able to remember the pairs of nouns. Students who construct images are better able to recall the content of prose passages. Students who attend to a lesson, for whatever reasons, are more likely to learn from it. Knowledge about the mediational process of attending helps us interpret the findings that teachers who are enthusiastic or gesture or move around are more effective.

This criticism of the process–product paradigm can be accommodated if that paradigm is elaborated into a *teaching-process* ⟶ *student-process* ⟶ *student-product* paradigm. Then the student-process, or mediating-process, variables should become as much the focus of our concern as the teacher's behavior or process. For it is the student's responses or processes that bring about his learning or achievement.

Doyle also held that, since many different teacher behaviors can result in the same student processes or responses, we should not be surprised that many different kinds of teacher behavior seem to have the same kinds of effects on achievement. This apparent anomaly may disappear, since the different kinds of teacher behavior have in common the effect of bringing about the same kinds of student responses (mediating processes).

In short, the mediating-process paradigm does not so much replace the process–product paradigm as expand it. It tells the teacher and the research worker alike that special attention should be paid to the ways in which teacher behavior affects students' responses, behaviors, mediating processes, and activities — including the pupil's attending, being interested, persisting, comprehending, being active, participating, having a favorable attitude, performing homework, and being engaged in seatwork — all as they are manifested in the moment-to-moment, hour-by-hour, and day-to-day life of the classroom. The teacher and the researcher should not be concerned only with how teaching behavior affects achievement and attitudes at the end of a unit or course of instruction.

Many student mediating processes may be determined by factors and agents other than the teacher's behaviors and decisions. But the teacher is the primary agent by which society can influence these determiners of what students learn. Hence, in research aimed at improving teaching and learning, it seems advantageous to work through that agent. Thus concern with improving mediating processes leads us back to concern with the process part of the process–product paradigm: teaching behavior.

The Classroom-Ecology Paradigm. As another supplement to the process–product paradigm, Doyle sees promise in what he calls the classroom-ecology paradigm. Here one focuses on the relationships between environmental demands and the human responses that occur in natural classroom settings. Research workers in this tradition have produced ethnographically "thick" descriptions — that is, descriptions full of the interpretation of events and processes embedded within a complex network of meanings.

From these descriptions, says Doyle, investigators have formulated the major task of the pupils in the classroom as *the exchange of performance for grades*. The classroom environment is complex. It consists of much oral discourse. As seen by any given pupil, it contains many other students, one or more adults, and a wide variety of materials. All of these provide competing sources of information. How can the pupil know what to do in order to get good grades?

Their descriptions have led the ethnographers to conclude that the cues available to pupils on this question are often unstated, inconsistent, incomplete, or even misleading. The cues change from class to class, from subject to subject, and from teacher to teacher. So pupils need to develop sophisticated techniques for determining what they should do and how well they are doing it. These techniques include a kind of "differential attentiveness." For example, the pupils may learn that teacher criticism may be more accurate than teacher praise as a cue to desirable performance. The pupils may also learn about many sources of cues other than the teacher, such as other students, textbooks, test questions and grades, and the teacher's written comments on assignments. Further, the student must learn to be patient, because classes are long, students are many, and the teacher's attention is a scarce resource.

In short, Doyle's classroom-ecology paradigm implies that research workers should study the way students learn to use cues concerning performance expectations and to prefer certain cues — for example, tests — rather than others — for example, praise. We should also study the ways in which students learn to compensate for the inadequacy of some cues, such as their teacher's instructions, by searching elsewhere for useful cues, by recalling previously useful cues, or by restructuring available cues.

Again, in my view, the classroom-ecology paradigm does not replace or render obsolete the process–product paradigm. The teacher is the one primarily responsible for determining what goes on in the classroom and for enhancing its educational value. The classroom-ecology point of view suggests that teachers and research workers should pay careful attention to the kinds of cues that teachers provide in guiding their students toward successful exchanges of performance for grades. If the cues now provided by teachers are indeed unclear, ambiguous, inconsistent, unstable, and otherwise inadequate, the implication is that teachers ought to do better and that research should be aimed at helping them do better. Cues are indeed available from sources other than the teacher, but research on *teacher* effectiveness must be concerned with what teachers do to affect the cues.

Thus, combined with the mediating-process paradigm, the classroom-ecology paradigm suggests a host of new variables worth investigating in relation to student acheivement and attitude, and as targets of teacher education aimed at improving teacher effectiveness. Pupils obtain cues not only from the teacher but also from textbooks, workbooks, films, tests, and other pupils. Teachers ought to learn how to manipulate these types of cue resources so as to help pupils understand better what they should do and how they should do it.

Doyle holds that teacher behaviors do not necessarily play a central role in defining performance expectations or in acquiring response capabilities. Hence there is little reason, from the ecological perspective, to anticipate that variations in these behaviors will be strongly related to mean gains in student achievement as conventionally measured in the process–product tradition. But Doyle seems thus to shift away from his own ostensible concern with paradigms for research on *teacher* effectiveness. He is turning instead to paradigms for research on any kind of determiner of student achievement. Suppose, however, we persist in a concern with teaching, because the teacher is the prime agent of society in influencing school learning. Then we must be concerned with the ways in which teachers could be made to play a more "central role" in defining performance expectations. We can alert teachers to the importance of such cues and devise ways in which teachers can exert greater control over them.

In short, Doyle's analysis leads to elaboration of the process–product paradigm rather than to its abandonment. The elaborated process–product paradigm would have four major links in the chain of categories of variables:

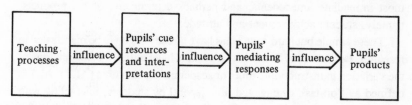

Process variables would still consist largely of the teacher behaviors that constitute methods, styles, strategies, techniques, and patterns of teaching. These teacher behaviors would in turn provide students with cues concerning the ways in which students can and should behave if they are to succeed in exchanging performance for a good grade. After the pupils have perceived and interpreted these cues, they will (with the teacher's help) exhibit the mediating responses, such as paying attention, getting interested, becoming active, using imagery and mnemonic devices, engaging in self-recitation, making responses, and attending to feedback. Finally, these student mediating responses will eventuate in the products — the kinds of achievement and attitudes that we have set up as the objectives of what goes on in the classroom.

If we wish to improve teaching as well as understand it, we must recognize the teacher as the prime agent of that improvement. This recognition means that the new kinds of variables called to our attention by new paradigms must be converted into types of teacher behavior — determined in turn by teacher concerns, policies, decisions, and habits. When that kind of conversion is made, the cue resources of the classroom-ecology paradigm and the pupil responses of the mediating-process paradigm are included in the concept of process. This inclusion leaves the process–product paradigm intact but enriched.

Instructional Time

Nevertheless, although the process–product paradigm remains intact, Doyle's critique suggests ways of looking more closely at the effects of teacher behavior. The expanded process–product paradigm implies that we should look most immediately at the effects of teacher behavior on the cues given students concerning how they should behave. It also implies that we should look at the effects of these cues on student behavior. Finally, it suggests that we also look at the way these student behaviors serve as the most immediate antecedents, and perhaps determiners, of the products, namely, student achievement and attitude.

These simple but hard-won ideas have already begun to be manifested in research. Berliner (1977) and his coworkers have initiated investigations of the variation in instructional time, or academic learning time (ALT). ALT is defined as "on-task or engaged time [spent] by students, interacting with materials or participating in activities of intermediate level difficulty, that are academically focussed" (p. 3).

The concept is traced by its authors to the formulations of learning and teaching by John B. Carroll, Benjamin S. Bloom, and the team of Annegret Harnischfeger and David Wiley. All of these writers have emphasized the importance of time as a factor in the learning process. If one focuses on academic achievement in, say, reading or mathematics as the product, then academic learning time should be expected to be the process variable that is necessary, even if not sufficient, for emergence of that product.

In a study of nine second-grade classes, the hypothesis that ALT would correlate with achievement (adjusted for the pupil's initial academic ability) was, in general, supported (Fisher, Filby, & Marliave, 1977). Nevertheless, "substantial differences in amounts of time were necessary before this relationship could be detected." Moreover, "the strength and consistency of the relationship varied considerably." These results indicate that differences in ALT alone will probably be far from adequate to account for differences in achievement. There is ample room for other variables in pupil activity — variables that remain to be identified as determiners of pupil achievement.

The kinds of recommendations that were illustrated in Chapter I may be regarded as pedagogical approaches resulting in "direct instruction." Such direct instruction seeks to maximize academic learning time. But differences in academic learning time alone seem insufficient, even though meaningful, to account for differences in achievement.

In what other directions should investigators turn their attention? Academic learning time, in the form of allocated and engaged learning time, is, in a sense, a psychologically empty quantitative concept. We need better analyses of how that time is filled, of what learning processes go on during academic learning time.

Filling In the Time

To formulate the variables and processes that should be observed and measured within academic learning time is to engage in the hypothesis-generating phases of our task. The approaches that suggest themselves here include those based on types of learning, analyses of teaching methods, analyses of subject matter and curricular objectives, and studies of student characteristics. Each of these domains suggests a variety of approaches to promising new variables.

Types of Learning. For example, types of learning include respondent learning, contiguity learning, operant conditioning, observational learning, and cognitive learning (Gage & Berliner, 1975, pp. 87–161). *Respondent learning* occurs when a stimulus, when paired with another that elicits an emotional response, itself becomes capable of eliciting a very similar response. The teacher hugging the kindergartener on the first day of school hopes to bring forth respondent learning. *Contiguity learning* occurs when the placing of stimuli close to one another in time or space makes one of the stimuli able to call forth the other as a response. The teacher using flash cards in class drill is exploiting this principle by having pupils hear the correct response follow closely upon the flashed card. *Operant conditioning* — perhaps the most influential conception of learning during the 1950s and 1960s — tells us that certain stimuli that follow upon a response can reinforce, or strengthen, the response. The teacher thus gives favorable attention to the pupils who are working on their assignment. *Observational learning* takes place when we learn from merely looking at or listening to a respected model whose complex behavior we can emulate. The instructor at the wheel of the driver education car and the teacher at the blackboard writing the letter *q* are teaching on the basis of observational learning. The same kind of teaching goes on as children watch heroes and villains on television. Finally, *cognitive learning* occurs as we process information through a set of structures including receptors, a sensory register, a short-term memory, a long-term memory from which information can be retrieved by a search which returns it to the short-term memory. The information then activates a response generator, which is governed by executive control processes and expectancies (Gagné, 1976). The lecturer or textbook author is teaching by means of such processes, and he uses logical content structures to do so.

The point here is that no single kind of learning can be expected to account for all the learning — and teaching — that goes on. Different kinds of things are learned in different ways (Gage, 1972, pp. 40–83). The processes that go on during academic learning time consist of the processes that go on during respondent, contiguity, operant, observational, or cognitive learning. Fruitful new hypotheses concerning teaching will emerge from examination of the implications of those conceptions of learning.

Teaching Methods. Similarly, we should not ignore what we have learned from both ancient and recent teaching methods. Whatever their relative merits, none of these teaching methods is completely unsuccessful. The fact that students learn at all from lecturing, for example, is important — even if, as has traditionally been argued, students do not learn as well from this method as from others. The same is true of other teaching methods: class discussion, tutoring, use of printed materials in seatwork and homework, computer-assisted instruction, simulations and games, and television or film (see Gage, 1976). Each of these can contribute ingredients of the process called classroom instruction. The proportions of those ingredients that make up any teacher's ways of classroom teaching will influence what goes on during academic learning time. Do the students answer questions in the printed materials? What kinds of questions — lower-order or higher-order? Do the questions precede or follow the didactic material? These queries illustrate the many kinds of variables suggested by a detailed consideration of teaching methods.

A picture begins to emerge: Teaching that leads optimally to knowledge and understanding of complex tasks or materials — as in reading, mathematics, chemistry, or French — must meet intricate requirements (which have been or might be revealed by research on the learning and teaching of such subjects) relative to the proper sequencing and elaboration of concepts, instances, principles, and problems.

For example, in learning to read, fourth-grade children have acquired the ability to identify words not previously encountered, by using rules that relate printed letters to speech sounds. One factor in this rule learning process is the complexity of the letter–sound correspondence rules (Guthrie & Seifert, 1977). Thus,

> the simple patterns are detected and abstracted before more complex patterns or rules. For instance, the checked alternates of the vowels are governed by fairly simple rules. The vowel is mapped directly to a sound in c*at*, b*et*, p*in*, c*ot*, and c*ut*. However, more complex rules are needed to handle the free alternates (pine, cute), the secondary vowel patterns (bait, bead), and the consonant-influenced vowels (wild, post) (p. 687).

Knowledge of this kind is too intricate to be used by teachers in the give-and-take of classroom discourse (although it might ideally be understood by teachers); but it can be used in developing the reading materials and work sheets used by their pupils.

Similar examples of how research throws light on the proper sequencing of tasks and the optimal teaching of concepts and principles could be cited in other subject matters. Thus, Klausmeier, Ghatala, and Frayer (1974) formulated a three-step instructional design for the teaching of concepts: (1) analyzing the concept by providing its definition, relevant and irrelevant attributes, and examples and nonexamples; (2) specifying the level at which the concept is to be attained (concrete, identity, classificatory, or formal) and the cognitive operations underlying that attainment; and (3) identifying the appropriate instructional strategies. In two studies, the design was applied in teaching the concept "equilateral triangle" to fourth graders and the concept "tree" to third graders. Again, it is noteworthy that this approach had to be incorporated into *written* instructional lessons (McMurray, Bernard, Klausmeier, Schilling, & Vorwerk, 1977, p. 661).

The role of the teacher then becomes one that is aimed at bringing the students into effective interaction with the instructional materials, with a maximum of engaged academic learning time. Effective teachers can thus work almost equally well in all subject matters, at least at the elementary school level, because their knowledge of the subject matter need be adequate only to the task of supplementing the instructional materials with which the students are working. Even at the secondary school level, the teacher's role becomes generally the same across subject matters because the complexities specific to teaching the particular subject are handled by the instructional materials. In other words: the effective teacher becomes in substantial degree a humane facilitator of student interaction with instructional material; thus the kinds of "teaching skills" that are most effective in helping students use specialized "teaching materials" will always be needed and appropriate, regardless of subject matter.

Subject Matter and Objectives. If different kinds of things are learned in different ways, different subject matters and curricular objectives should call upon different kinds of learning and teaching. If this be so, we should look at the properties of different subject matters and objectives. Analysis of the content of second-grade reading instruction, for example, has identified decoding, context clues, word structure, word meaning, comprehension, and reading practice tasks, among others. Decoding can be analyzed into that which deals with single consonants, consonant blends and digraphs, variant consonants, short vowels, long vowels, vowel digraphs, vowel diphthongs, silent letters, and the like (Fisher, Filby, & Marliave, 1977). Instructional materials, much more than teachers, must be relied upon to provide proper coverage of all these complex matters. History, science, mathematics, and languages can be similarly analyzed. And the results will yield clues about the student activities entailed in coping with the tasks revealed by such analyses. In turn, the student activities will suggest the kinds of cues that teachers should provide through their own behavior in explaining, making assignments, and organizing the classroom's activity.

Student Characteristics. Finally, student characteristics suggest clues to the significant processes that should fill academic learning time. The most frequently considered characteristic is intelligence, or general scholastic aptitude. According to Glaser (1977), "Verbal aptitude and ability are related to the rapidity of information processing in memory" (p. 61); hence, it becomes profitable to determine whether we can "identify situations where speed and other properties of such processing can be taken into account to facilitate school achievement'' (p. 61). Similarly, consideration of adaptation to student anxiety (Peterson, 1976), of teachers' and students' beliefs about the behavioristic or humanistic character of psychology (Majasan, 1972), of students' tendencies to seek achievement through independence or conformance (Domino, 1971) may yield hypotheses concerning significant dimensions of teaching. In short, certain characteristics of students have been found to interact with the ways in which students are taught. Research on these interactions (Cronbach & Snow, 1977) may throw light on the dimensions of teaching that make a difference in student learning.

The National Conference on Studies in Teaching

Assistance with the substantive issues of research on teaching was provided by several of the panels of the National Conference on Studies in Teaching conducted in 1974 by the National Institute of Education. Five of the ten panels dealt with teaching as, respectively, human interaction, behavior analysis, skill performance, a linguistic process in a cultural setting, and clinical information processing. (Other panels dealt with teacher recruitment, selection, and retention; instructional personnel utilization; personnel roles in new instructional systems; research methodology; and theory development.) Each of these formulations emphasized a particular facet of teaching. The reports contain statements of the approaches, programs, and projects considered by each panel to be promising.

Thus, the Panel on Teaching as Human Interaction formulated one approach intended to "develop knowledge and understanding of human interaction within educational settings." Within that approach, one program was intended to "develop new ways to conceptualize and analyze patterns of teacher–pupil interaction." Within that program, one project was intended to "design and create the capability of establishing a data bank of recorded interactive behavior complete with associated paper-and-pencil test data," and another project was designed to "examine the cycles of development through which interaction patterns mature."

These panel reports abound in ideas for research on teaching. The panel report on "Teaching as Clinical Information Processing" provided the basis for the Institute for Research on Teaching established at Michigan State University in 1976. The panel report on "Teaching as a Linguistic Process in a Cultural Setting" seems likely to eventuate in research projects supported by the National Institute of Education. Thus, efforts are under way to act upon the formulations and conceptions underlying the National Conference and at least some of its panels.

The Teacher's Implicit Theory of Teaching

One additional substantive direction for research on teaching is worth mentioning. It takes the form of concern with what might be called the teacher's implicit theory of teaching. The theory is implicit because the teacher could probably not be readily articulate about it. The theory takes the form of a hierarchically structured set of beliefs about the proper ends and means of teaching, the characteristics of students, the modes of learning, and the ways in which all of these interact to govern the teacher's behavior at any given moment. This implicit theory enables the teacher to cope with the otherwise overwhelming abundance of problematic situations or occasions for decision making that confront a teacher moment by moment during a school day. Because teachers do not have time for deliberation or elaborate reasoning processes in the heat of their interaction with students, they must fall back upon general principles and guidelines that they have more or less consciously adopted.

Such implicit theories are easier to illustrate at the more specific levels. One example would be the general principle that the difficulty level of the second task should be a function of the student's performance on a first task; the less well the student does, the easier the next task should be (Beavin, 1970). Another example would be a tendency to tell a pupil that a problem is easy. The tutor or teacher intends such a statement to encourage the pupil to try, but it may have the undesirable effect of making success with the problem less rewarding and failure all the more discouraging. A third example is the highly prevalent tendency to praise pupils' responses. Teachers here seem to be operating with a reinforcement theory that says praise will get pupils to try more often, but the effect may be to make pupils so accustomed to praise that it loses its effectiveness (not to mention the ultimately confusing effect of praising poor or faulty responses). A fourth tendency is to ask lower-order questions that require simple recall of information already heard or read. Here, teachers seem to assume that knowledge is important as the basis for higher levels of achievement. Or they may believe that complex reasoning cannot properly be expected in the midst of classroom discourse. In any case, as we have seen, research tends to support this tendency of teachers.

These simple maxims of teacher conduct ought to be explored. They can be organized into larger structures of implicit theory concerned with such matters as the formulation of objectives, the comprehension of the student's initial state of readiness, the organization and administration of classroom activity, the selection and use of explanation and questioning and reacting, and the proper use of tests. Teachers must inevitably make decisions on these matters. Their decisions cumulate into overall conceptions of their own role, the role of the student, and the nature of education.

Ways of eliciting the teacher's implicit theory come readily to mind. We could begin with broad and unstructured interviews that would allow the teachers to formulate the basic dimensions of their conceptions of teaching and their positions on those dimensions. Gradually, the interviews would move toward greater specificity. Finally, to fill in gaps that had been left by the teacher and the interviewer, detailed questionnaires could be used. As this process was repeated with successive groups of teachers, the interviews and the questionnaires would become more adequate. Eventually, it would become possible to map the implicit theories of teachers in a well-organized way. The theories described would range from high-level abstractions to the rules teachers use to govern their most specific acts.

Connections between the teacher's beliefs and classroom behaviors could then be investigated. The ways in which behavior accords with belief would be described. We would give special attention to the ways in which behavior departs from the the teacher's previously expressed convictions. The departures would lay bare the implicit reasoning that leads teachers to make exceptions to their own rules. These exceptions could then be used to refine the description of the teacher's belief system.

In this way, teachers and research workers could collaborate toward a conception of teaching based in detail on what teachers themselves know and believe about their work. The gap between "knowledge that" and "knowledge how" would be reduced. Teacher training would turn away from an overreliance on performance skills in areas where behavior is governed less by skill than by belief. For example, to ask the right kinds of questions probably depends less on a skill that needs to be practiced than on a distinction that needs to be understood. Research on teachers' cognitive structures concerning teaching would bear upon this possibility.

METHODOLOGICAL ISSUES

The methods of describing, measuring, and interrelating the phenomena of teaching also need to be reconsidered as we undertake to improve the scientific basis of the art of teaching. The prevalent methods have recently been challenged. We need to consider the criticism of those methods and the substitutes and supplements that have been proposed.

"Qualitative" versus "Quantitative" Approaches

Most research on teaching until now has used the methods of behavioral scientists — primarily psychologists and sociologists. These methods have included techniques of observation, testing, and statistical analysis in all their well-known forms. The typical project has used observation schedules to describe and measure the behavior of teachers and their pupils, psychological tests to measure the initial abilities and aptitudes of the pupils, achievement tests and attitude inventories to measure the outcomes of the teaching–learning process, and statistical methods such as correlation and analysis of covariance to show how processes are related to products and to each other.

Recently, this "paradigm" has been challenged (Tikunoff & Ward, 1977). Anthropologists and linguists have proposed "qualitative" methods — methods that "challenge the presuppositions of the natural science approach to scientific investigation" (Rist, 1977, p. 44).

Qualitative approaches take an inner as well as an outer perspective on human behavior. The inner perspective is attainable only through trying to participate in the life of the other person and seeking insights through introspection. Qualitative methods include participant observation, in-depth interviewing, full participation in the processes being examined, field work, and the like — all aimed at giving the investigator first-hand experience with what he is studying. The approach leads to concern with "frequently minute episodes or interactions that are examined for broader patterns and processes" (p. 44). The qualitative researcher tries to interpret the world from the point of view of the persons being studied. "The canons and precepts of the scientific method are seen to be insufficient; what are needed are intersubjective understandings" (p. 44).

In practice, the qualitative approach leads to careful descriptions of what goes on in classrooms and schools. The descriptions are rich in detail and interpretaion. The qualitative research worker seeks to understand causality without breaking down reality into its component parts.

Viehoever (1976) has identified a set of issues on which the quantitative and qualitative approaches tend to differ: The qualitative methodologist, in addition to focusing intensively on single events or situations, emphasizes subjective phenomena, carries out nondirected observation, prefers inductive strategies and heuristics, emphasizes the situational context, observes performance in the natural setting rather than the test situation, rejects sophisticated statistical analysis and randomized designs, emphasizes divergent rather than convergent realities, and uses popularized and affect-laden terminology.

It seems unlikely that either the qualitative or the quantitative research worker will accept the other as a replacement. Rist (1977) hopes for a movement "from disdain to détente." Beyond détente, we should hope for mutual exploitation of findings. Each kind of investigator should benefit from what the other reports.

"Quantitative" researchers can use the insights achieved through ethnography and linguistic analysis, through intensive study of the hidden and subjective meanings of a single phenomenon, to formulate and observe phenomena and variables that they might otherwise ignore. They should realize that a single occurrence of a phenomenon, observed by an ethnographer or linguist or connoisseur, is sufficient to prove that that phenomenon is *possible*.

But "qualitative" investigators should realize that their data as such are inadequate to determine the degree to which the phenomenon is *probable*. The question of probability can be determined only by the analysis of frequencies of occurrence in a sample of observations. Such analysis requires counting, samples, unambiguous measures, and statistics.

Similarly, if the ethnographer observes that one kind of event seems to cause another, he or she can infer merely the possiblity that the two events are causally connected. A stronger basis in inductive inference for drawing conclusions about cause-and-effect relationships can be obtained only through the study of a number of events or phenomena — a study that thus becomes "quantitative."

Finally, it is important to note that the two kinds of research operate in different contexts — the context of discovery and the context of justification. The qualitative researcher can *discover* new phenomena and relationships or create new hypotheses. The quantitative researcher is better able to test, validate, or *justify* the hypotheses.

> The act of discovery escapes logical analysis: there are no logical rules in terms of which a "discovery machine" could be constructed that would take over the creative function of the genius. But it is not the logician's task to account for scientific discoveries; all he can do is to analyze the relations between given facts and a theory presented to him with the claim that it explains these facts. In other words, logic [like quantitative research] is concerned only with the context of justification (Reichenbach, 1951, p. 231).

The Descriptive-Correlational-Experimental Loop

Most of the studies of teaching performed within the process–product paradigm have been correlational studies. As is well known, such studies describe relationships between variables measured as they occur under natural conditions. Apart from their advantage in making possible the relatively easy analysis of the relationships between fairly large numbers of variables in a single study, correlational studies have the serious disadvantage of making cause–effect interpretations hazardous. It cannot be known with any assurance that a teacher behavior that correlates with a kind of pupil achievement is the cause of that pupil achievement.

For this reason, many writers, such as Rosenshine and Furst (1973) and Dunkin and Biddle (1974), have spoken of the "descriptive-correlational-experimental loop":

> The paradigm contains at least these elements:
> 1. development of procedures for describing teaching in a quantitative manner;
> 2. correlational studies in which the descriptive variables are related to measures of student growth;
> 3. experimental studies in which the significant variables obtained in the correlational studies are tested in a more controlled stiuation (Rosenshine & Furst, 1973, p. 122).

We know that the first two elements listed above have been performed in considerable abundance. Literally hundreds of *descriptive* instruments have been developed, and for the most part applied, as exemplifications of the first element (Simon & Boyer, 1970).

Similarly, many *correlational* studies have been performed. Moreover, the number of such studies seems to be growing ever more rapidly. Rosenshine was able to locate only about fifty such studies in the review he published in 1971. But Dunkin and Biddle were able to report on more than one hundred in 1974. Since then the number has greatly increased. Moreover, the scale and sophistication of these correlational studies have also increased. No longer is the work limited to what can be done in doctoral dissertations, which constituted the bulk of such studies until about a decade ago.

By the logic of the descriptive-correlational-experimental loop, the next stage should be one in which *experiments* are carried out. And, indeed, such experiments are being performed — not in large numbers and not on grand scales but at least in accordance with the reasoning that, once we have identified types of teacher behavior that correlate with student achievement and attitude, we should proceed to manipulate these types of teacher behavior to determine whether they do in fact have a causal influence. If the causal connection is demonstrated, the experiment will have yielded clear implications for teacher education. The implications are that anyone who wants to improve the effect of teacher behavior on student achievement or attitude should help teachers to behave in the ways exemplified by the levels of the independent variable that yielded the most desirable values of student achievement and attitude.

Objections to Experiments in Classrooms

Yet experiments on teaching have not been regarded with unquestioning enthusiasm. Some investigators have raised a host of objections against the feasibility and desirability of such experiments. I should like to consider at least some of these objections, especially in the light of an experiment conducted at Stanford University.

First, it is argued that randomization, or random assignment of subjects to treatments, is not feasible except in laboratories. Not so. This procedure was successfully carried out in two school districts near Stanford University, with the consent of volunteer teachers, who accepted the explanation that such random assignment to trained and untrained groups was necessary if the proposed experiment was to yield the scientific knowledge at which the research was aimed.

A second difficulty in experimentation can arise when a pretest has stimulated such interest in the content of the experimental teaching that some teachers supplement the experimental materials with additional charts, models, pamphlets, and discussions. But, when teachers were carefully informed and instructed as to the nature of the experiment being conducted, they were able and willing to conform to its requirements. Observations and interviews with the teachers in the Stanford experiment revealed no substantial violations of the research requirements. Indeed, the teachers in the experimental and control groups were asked not to communicate with any other teacher concerning the content of the teacher training received by the experimental groups. Interviews, observations, and incidental evidence indicate that almost all of the teachers have adhered to this prohibition of communication. In any case, it was possible, through detailed and frequent observation of the teachers in all of the groups before, during, and after the

teacher training, to determine whether the control group adopted any of the
teacher behaviors recommended to the experimental groups. The observations will thus provide a relatively objective indication of the degree to
which the control group was, so to speak, "contaminated." When scientific
requirements are carefully explained, the public is likely to accept experiments. That acceptance was found by Hillis and Wortman (in press) in the
case of college students' reactions to a randomized control-group design in a
medical experiment.

A third problem affecting classroom experiments is the occurrence of an
unexpected interruption. In the Stanford experiment, the interruption was a
teachers' strike. During the strike, neither observation of the classrooms nor
training of the teachers could be conducted. The duration of these activities
was accordingly curtailed. But, since the Stanford experiment was self-
contained within each school district, comparisons of the experimental and
control groups of classrooms within each district could still be valid. Only
generalizations from one school district to the next might be jeopardized.
Nevertheless, the degree to which cross-district comparability was disturbed
could be determined through observations, questionnaires, and interviews,
and thus could be taken into account.

A fourth objection is that experiments with teachers must depend on
volunteers, that is, teachers who are willing to be randomly assigned to
control and experimental groups and who are willing to take a teacher-training program if they are assigned to the experimental group. Yet the fact of
such dependence on volunteers is, in another sense, an advantage to the external validity, or relevance to the real world, of such an experiment. This is
so because inservice teacher education programs in many school districts
may need to be limited to teachers who are willing to undertake such
programs voluntarily.

Fifth, it is objected that the random assignment of children to control and
experimental groups is impossible, or at least difficult. But such random
assignment is unnecessary to the logic of classroom experimentation, where
the classroom is the unit of analysis and also the unit of random assignment.
If the teachers are willing to be randomly assigned to treatments, that is sufficient. Suppose stratified random assignment of teachers is carried out, with
strata formed on the basis of the mean level of initial measures of relevant
variables. Then the experimental and control groups of both teachers and
pupils should turn out to be nonsignificantly different with respect to the
relevant characteristics of both teachers and pupils.

Finally, we have the question of whether observers should remain neutral or yield to requests from students or teachers for help with classroom or subject matter problems. When the purposes of the research and observation have been adequately explained, teachers and pupils understand that the observers must remain neutral and refrain from becoming involved in classroom activities. In our experience, this role of the observer was readily understood and accepted by both teachers and pupils.

Thus we find that many objections raised against randomized control-group experiments in classrooms appear, in the light of actual experience with such an experiment, to be overdrawn, easily avoidable, or irrelevant. The literature on experiments of this kind is vast and sophisticated, and writers such as Barber (1976) and Cook and Campbell (1976), among others, have provided insightful and ingenious ways of overcoming the threats to the validity of such experiments.

In view of the relative dearth and the high value of experiments on teaching, we need such experiments. They will test the two crucial kinds of causal connections, namely, the connections between teacher education programs and teacher behavior, on the one hand, and the connections between teacher behavior and student achievement and attitude, on the other hand. Now that hundreds of correlational studies have been performed, we need experiments designed to take the next step in the descriptive-correlational-experimental loop. Their results will tell us whether we are ready to attempt truly justifiable changes in how teachers behave.

Intensive Experimental Designs

One resolution of the qualitative–quantitative issue can take the form of intensive experimental designs. Here we can gain the intimacy of contact with reality that the qualitative researcher values, while preserving the rigor and objectivity to which the quantitative investigator pays allegiance.

In an intensive experiment, the investigator substitutes frequency of observation for numbers of persons. He or she studies one or a few pupils, teachers, or classes but makes repeated observations of the single case or few cases before, during, and after some intervention.

The study of single cases has a long history in psychoanalysis, child study, medicine, and anthropology. In experimental psychology, it was developed primarily by B. F. Skinner and his disciples (see especially Sidman, 1960). Recently it has been used in the study of behavioral counseling (see Thoresen & Anton, 1974). In that kind of research, a single kind of behavior is counted on successive occasions—hours, days, or weeks. The trend of the frequencies is noted before, during, and after the interjection of a treatment. The treatment may then be withdrawn, reinstated, withdrawn again, and so on. What happens to the frequency of the given behavior tells the effectiveness of the treatment for the particular person or small number of persons treated. By inference to similar persons, we can gradually accumulate confidence in our judgment of the treatment's effectiveness in modifying the frequency of the behavior — whether it be bedwetting, speaking out of turn in class, smoking, or waking up in the middle of the night.

At first glance, the appropriateness of this kind of research seems to be limited to dependent variables of interest only as to their frequency. It is difficult to see how it can be used for dependent variables that are to be changed in level or quality. Research of this kind has not been conducted with dependent variables consisting of achievement of cognitive objectives. Such dependent variables include level of knowledge, depth of understanding, and difficulty of problems that can be solved. With this kind of variable we do not count the frequency of occurrences of the same kind of behavior, such as speaking out of turn; rather we measure the change in kind, or level, of achievement on a scale — for example, a scale ranging from complete ignorance of algebra to ability to solve difficult problems in algebra.

Can the advantages of intensive experiments be gained for research on teaching — research in which the dependent variable consists of level of achievement rather than frequency of occurrence? Unfortunately, it is difficult to substitute numbers of observations of a single student or class for a single observation (or test) of many students or classes. But it can be done, as the following example shows.

Suppose we wish to investigate the effect of structuring, as defined earlier — structuring that consists of the six components of reviewing the main idea, stating objectives, etc. The teacher develops such structuring for use in teaching a two-day unit on ecology. At the end of the unit, the teacher gives the class a test measuring the knowledge, understanding, and attitudes that were the objectives of the unit. Then the teacher conducts a two-day unit on seismology, *without* the structuring components, and gives a test aimed at *its* objectives. This procedure is followed over a sequence of perhaps eight units, in an $S s S s S s S s$ design — the S indicating a structured unit, the s an unstructured one. If percentages of correct or desirable responses on the successive unit tests are computed, and if the teacher's tests have norms based on the performance of other groups of students taught all units by the same method, the cumulative results will throw light on the effects of structuring for this teacher and this class. Thus, if the students of this one teacher consistently do better (have a higher mean percentile rank on the preestablished norms of the unit tests) when taught by S than by s, then we can infer that S is more effective for this teacher. Replicated with other teachers and classes, the experiment would reveal the generality of the effects of structuring over different teachers, classes, and subject matters.

The question may be raised: If the experiment is to be replicated eventually, why not replicate it at once, by conducting the same experiment simultaneously in the classes of 20 or 200 teachers? The answer is that successive rather than simultaneous replication permits focus on the details of process and product in a single class. It also permits the refinement of teaching and testing procedures on the basis of accumulated experience in successive units and classes.

Various intensive experimental designs have been highly developed for the study of behavior change in psychotherapy and behavioral counseling (Hersen & Barlow, 1976). This development has been accompanied by the growth of a body of statistical methods appropriate to such designs (Kazdin, 1976). The transfer of this methodological paradigm to research on teaching should yield important advances toward the ideals of both the qualitative and the quantitative research methodologies.

Path Analysis

At the other methodological extreme from intensive experiments is the method of path analysis, which is just beginning to be applied to research on teaching. Path analysis begins with a model showing the variables considered to be involved in producing variance in a given outcome, such as reading achievement. The variables are arranged in what the investigator considers to be, on external or a priori grounds, a causal sequence. For example, if one variable, such as a score on a scholastic aptitude test, precedes another variable, such as a score on an achievement test, this means that the former is posited as a cause of the latter. In general, chronological sequence guides assumptions about causal sequence. Similarly, correlational and experimental evidence from previous research can serve as a basis for causal inferences. Especially when correlational methods (such as partial correlation) are used for holding other variables constant, we have a better basis for hypothesizing a causal connection between two variables.

The need for path analysis has been well expressed by McGuire (1973), who held that the typical experiment operates on what may be

a simple linear process model, a sequential chain of cause and effect which is inadequate to simulate the true complexities of the individual's cognitive system or of the social system which we are typically trying to describe. Such simple *a*-affects-*b* hypotheses fail to catch the complexities of parallel processing, bidirectional causality, and reverberating feedback that characterize both cognitive and social organizations. The simple sequential model had its uses, but these have been largely exploited in past progress, and we must now deal with the complexities of systems in order to continue the program on a new level (p. 448).

What McGuire was saying about research in social psychology applies to research on teaching. We are capable of conceiving of more complex models than that which relates one independent variable to one dependent variable.

Path analysis has been applied to research on teaching by McDonald and Elias (1976). They set up a "structural" model that portrayed student learning as caused by student behavior and also by students' attitudes, cognitive style, verbal aptitude, and expectations. Student behavior in turn was portrayed as being caused by teaching performances. The latter were in turn shown as being determined by the teacher's aptitudes, knowledge of the subject, knowledge of teaching, expectations, and attitudes, and also by the organizational stucture of the school. The full model shows, by means of curved lines, correlations between various pairs of the student variables and also between various pairs of the teacher variables. Straight lines show hypothesized causal connections between pairs of variables, with an arrow pointing to the dependent variable.

Once the structural model has been made and hypotheses about causal connections have thus been stated, mathematical techniques are applied to the correlations among all the variables involved in the model. These techniques yield path coefficients that show the strength of the hypothesized causal relationships. The coefficients are based on partial correlations that hold other variables constant as each correlation between any two of the variables is estimated.

The results obtained by McDonald and Elias (1976) are too complex to be summarized here. They seem clearly to have demonstrated the usefulness and promise of path analysis. It is more profitable than sole reliance on correlations between teacher behavior variables and student achievement variables. The technique can throw light on the importance of variables, such as the student mediating processes discussed earlier, that logically should intervene between teacher behavior and pupil achievement. It can test in a systematic and interpretable way the validity of a conception of the postulated causal network connecting the variables. One must concur with McDonald and Elias when they "recommend that this approach to the analysis of data on teaching performance and student learning be used in future studies" (p. 943) and assert that such analyses "can in turn be the basis for developing more formal theories of teaching" (p. 944).

THE PROSPECT OF RESEARCH ON TEACHING

The mere attempt to sketch new approaches — substantive and methodological — implies an optimistic view of the prospects of research on teaching. As I argued in Chapter I, previous research has not proved to be altogether barren of a scientific basis for the art of teaching. As I argued in Chapter II, methods of applying that basis have not turned out to be unattainable. And in this chapter, we have seen that promising ideas about ways to enhance the next round of effort can readily be thought of.

This view is not universally shared. Some writers regard such optimism as vacuous and blind. They hold that the complexities of teaching have been shown to be intractable. Any hope of mastering these complexities is forlorn — doomed to founder in a morass of higher-and-higher-order interactions, historical relativisms that make today's truth tomorrow's falsehood, laws of learning that fail to hold, and profound misconceptions of the character of what the behavioral sciences can properly aspire to.

Thus, we are told, the best we can hope for is not prediction and control but mere temporary understanding. Humankind and teachers and schools will change, but probably not for the better. Even if the change is for the better, it will not be so because of any scientific effort.

It is tempting to interpret such melancholy in human terms. Perhaps one's style of work makes the difference. Nonexperimenters can more readily afford pessimism. Almost by definition, experimenters must be optimists. To try a new treatment, a new independent variable, requires and creates hope. Mere observers can indulge themselves in an above-the-battle contemplation of what seems like human folly.

Such a stylistic basis for explaining *weltschmerz* about research on teaching cannot, of course, be adequate. We must have other bases for seeing brighter prospects, and one basis is the long sweep of history. Pessimism as well as optimism can be blind. We can overlook the fallibility of predictions of failure just as easily as we can focus on their accuracy. In October

1903 (three months before the Wright brothers' first flight), the distin-
guished mathematician and astronomer, Simon Newcomb (1903), proved
conclusively that a heavier-than-air flying machine was impossible. Astronomer Forest Ray Moulton flatly predicted in 1935 that "there is not the
slightest possibility of such journeys [from Earth to the moon]" (quoted in
Garfield, 1977).

In medicine, anyone writing in the 1930s could have lamented the
therapeutic fruitlessness of the preceding sixty years of research on microbes
and microbial diseases. Medicine still had no cures for lobar pneumonia,
tuberculosis, syphilis, scarlet fever, typhoid, typhus fever, and a host of
other microbial diseases. But by 1976 that sixty-year period could be seen in
perspective:

> Penicillin did not simply drop into our laps in the mid 1930s nor did sulfa-
> nilamide. These agents, and their successors, could not have been dreamed
> of in the 1930s or now had it not been for the preceding sixty years of
> steady, intense, and often brilliant basic research which established first off
> that there were such things as microbes and microbial diseases and then
> succeeded in sorting out the various infectious diseases by name so that we
> knew with certainty which ones were caused by which bacteria or virus.
> This astonishing body of work . . . represents a landmark advance in human
> affairs (Thomas, 1976, p. 24).

Research on teaching may well be in a stage similar to the sixty-year pre-
penicillin stage of medicine — one in which the necessary knowledge and
understanding must accumulate so that breakthroughs can be exploited.

Another example of the way in which research can influence stalled
movements can be seen in the history of feminism. After American women
won the right to vote in 1920, nothing more seemed to happen. One can
marvel at the advancement and foresight of a Lucy Stone in the 1830s and
also wonder why her ideas had no strong impact until the 1960s. One
answer is that the behavioral sciences had to develop to make her doctrine
widely understandable and accepted. We had to learn about cultural relati-
vism, role theory, and the acquired character of many socially significant
sex differences. These ideas helped initiate the new surge toward the libera-
tion of women. But a social thinker writing in the 1930s might well have
asserted that women had already gone about as far as they could go toward
equal status, just as many writers today see no prospect of any research-
based improvement of teaching.

Even if research is considered worth doing, there is disagreement on
whether the research should be focused on problems or, on the other hand,
try to be "basic." Some achievements of science and technology are seren-

dipitous; others result from a single-minded, direct attack on a practical problem. Penicillin illustrates the former, the airplane the latter. In research on teaching the same will probably be true. Some of our advances may grow out of research on matters as far afield as Bayesian theory in statistics or artificial intelligence in computer science. Others will result from direct attempts to answer the question *How should I teach?* If the direct attack on problems of teaching should have no monopoly on the effort to realize the promise of research for education, neither should it be demeaned. We should, of course, look for indirect help from research on cognitive development, the reading process, the brain and neural processes, cultural pluralism, school environments, and other matters only obliquely related to ways of teaching (Kiesler & Turner, 1977, pp. 19–43). But we should also not hesitate to look straight at the problems of teaching.

The prospect that lies before research on teaching is one in which more effective kinds of teacher behavior will gradually emerge from the experiments just beginning to be conducted. Those experiments will yield some main effects that will have general value for all teaching, whatever the grade level, subject matter, or character of the student. Other findings will reveal that certain other ways of teaching prove superior only for certain combinations of grade level, subject matter, and student characteristics. Probably none of the generalizations that survive the test of experimentation will permit highly exact prediction or unerring control of educational results. Nonetheless, they will improve substantially on the unaided common sense or raw experience of the teacher.

The research findings will dampen much of the oscillation of educational fashion — between progressivism and traditionalism, open education and direct instruction, heuristic and didactic teaching. None of these ways of teaching will pass from the scene, but they will be used with better understanding of the value each can help achieve. Controversies over purposes will persist. If and when they are resolved, however, we shall be better justified in our choice of teaching methods by which to realize our values.

At least for the foreseeable future, research on teaching will proceed as "normal science" (Kuhn, 1962); that is, investigators will follow the elaborated process–product paradigm and work on cleaning up an enormous number of details in the unfinished business of the field. New variables will be identified, invented, and measured. More ingenious ways of relating the variables, especially in complex causal patterns, will be devised and exploited. Better qualitative investigations, more comprehensive correlational studies, more intensive and single-case experiments, and more comprehensive path analyses will be performed. Better meta-analyses will bring together the results of the research in more valid and interpretable ways.

Within the field of teacher education, the knowledge of better ways to teach will be applied more effectively. The applications will be more warmly welcomed because teachers will have much greater say in determining the substance, method, and organization of the education. The voice of teachers on these matters will be more enlightened because they will have understood and shared in developing, through collaboration with research workers, the scientific basis for the objectives and methods of teacher education programs.

None of these changes will diminish the need for artistry in teaching. Like physicians and engineers, teachers will need to go beyond the scientific basis as they go about their work. Each student will present problems to which the strong generalizations, the qualified principles, and the weak suppositions will need to be applied with intelligence and judgment. Just as the physician tells almost every patient not to smoke, so the teacher will see to it that almost every pupil has adequate academic learning time. But just as the physician occasionally tells a tobacco addict that smoking is preferable to gaining twenty pounds, so the teacher may cut down the academic learning time of the occasional pupil who needs to learn to work under pressure. Just as the weak but steadily improving correlations between risk factors and heart disease have become important tools in the fight against premature death, so the weak but steadily improving connections between teaching patterns and educational outcomes will become more useful tools in the war against ignorance and alienation. Research on teaching promises no millennium; it merely holds out a reasonable prospect of improving on the way teaching is.

APPENDIX

Tables Showing Tests
of the Significance of Combined Results

TABLE A. *Teacher Indirectness and Pupil Achievement, Field Surveys*

TABLE B. *Teacher Indirectness and Student Achievement, Field Surveys: Alternative Findings for Three Methods of Combining the Results Shown in Table A*

TABLE C. *Teacher Praise and Pupil Attitudes*

TABLE D. *Teacher Acceptance of Pupils' Ideas and Pupil Achievement*

TABLE E. *Teacher Acceptance of Pupils' Ideas and Pupil Achievement: Alternative Findings for Three Methods of Combining the Results Shown in Table D*

TABLE F. *Teacher Criticism and Disapproval and Student Achievement*

TABLE G. *Teacher Criticism and Disapproval and Student Achievement: Alternative Findings for Three Methods of Combining the Results Shown in Table F*

TABLE A
Teacher Indirectness and Pupil Achievement, Field Surveys (Based on Dunkin and Biddle, 1974, p. 115)

Study	Duration of Teaching	Grade Level	No. of Teachers	Definition of Independent Variable	Definition of Dependent Variable	Result	Probability of Result	χ^2	Equivalent r Obtained by Glass et al. (1977)
Flanders (1970)	2 semesters	2	15	Factor I ($i/i + d$)	"Portions of a nationally standardized achievement test covering language and number skills were used to form a composite score" (p. 393)	$r = -.073$	.605	1.0051	$r = -.073$
Flanders (1970)	2 weeks	4	16	ditto	Achievement test covering a two-week unit in social studies	$r = .308$	.123	4.1911	$r = .308$
Flanders (1970)	2 semesters	6	30	ditto	Metropolitan Achievement Test mean score	$r = .224$	.142	3.9039	$r = .224$
Flanders (1970)	2 weeks	7	15	ditto	Special social studies unit on New Zealand	$r = .481$	.035	6.7048	$r = .481$
Flanders (1970)	2 weeks	8	16	ditto	Special mathematics unit dealing with applications of algebraic and geometric formulas	$r = .428$	.049	6.0319	$r = .428$

Study	Duration		n	Instrument	Outcome measure	Statistic	p	Value	r
Cook (1967)	2 semesters	10	8	Flanders I/D ratio (pp. 26, 27)	Watson-Glaser Critical Thinking Appraisal	$\chi^2 = 13.33$, $df = 7$	.067	5.4061	$r = .09$
					Processes of Science Test	$\chi^2 = 9.55$, $df = 7$	.217	3.0557	$r = .07$
					Comprehensive Final Test	$\chi^2 = 9.55$, $df = 7$	.217	3.0557	$r = .07$
Furst (1967)	4 one-hour lessons	10, 12	15	40-minute achievement test on international economic problems (Same as Bellack et al., 1966) Three groups consisting of 3 high-achieving, 8 average, and 4 low-achieving classes (See Footnote a)	Composite of three Flanders variables: (a) ratio of extended indirect teacher influence to extended direct teacher influence; (b) revised i/d in response to pupil talk; (c) extended student talk	$F = 3.895$ $df = 2, 12$	.024	7.4594	$r = .11$ $r = .26$
Medley & Mitzel (1959)	2 semesters	3–6	49	"Emotional Climate" as measured by OScAR (p. 241)	Four subtests of the California Reading Test (elementary): word form, word recognition, meaning of similarities, and interpretation of meanings	$r = .20$	.081	5.0266	$r = .20$
Powell (1968)	2 semesters	3	9	See Footnote b	SRA Achievement Series: Composite	$F = 5.85$ $df = 1,164$	.007	9.9237	$r = .23$
					SRA Reading Total	$F = 1.30$, $df = 1,164$	.127	4.1271	$r = .11$
					SRA Arithmetic Total	$F = 10.68$ $df = 1,164$	.001	13.8155	$r = .31$

TABLE A   Continued

Study	Duration of Teaching	Grade Level	No. of Teachers	Definition of Independent Variable	Definition of Dependent Variable	Result	Probability of Result	x^2	Equivalent r Obtained by Glass et al. (1977)
Snider (1966)	2 semesters	12	17	Flanders $I/I + D$ Ratio: Five most direct teachers were compared with the five least direct teachers	New York Regents Physics Examination	Mann-Whitney $U = 18$	.155	3.7287	$r = .29$
					Cooperative Physics Test	$U = 13$	.500	1.3863	$r = .00$
					Test of Understanding Science-I	$U = 12$	.500	1.3863	$r = .00$
					Test of Understanding Science (total)	$U = 14$	.421	1.7302	$r = .06$
Weber (1968)	3 years	4	26	Classification of teacher on the basis of multivariate composite scores in Flanders Interaction Analysis Categories: 4 groups of pupils ($n = 45$ each) formed as follows: First 3 years had indirect teacher, 4th year indirect teacher; First 3 years indirect teacher, 4th year direct teacher; First 3 years direct teacher,	Torrance Test of Creative Thinking, verbal fluency score	For comparison of students who in 1st 3 years had indirect teachers vs. direct teachers, $F = 10.58$, $df = 1,176$	.001	13.8155	$r = .30$

Study	Duration	Grade	Teacher measure	Outcome measure	Statistic			r
Thompson & Bowers (1968)	2 semesters	4	teacher; First 3 years direct teacher; 4th year direct teacher — Teacher supportiveness (similar to "emotional climate" of the Medley-Mitzel OScAR-2e)	Stanford Achievement Test Vocabulary score	F < 1.0 df = 1, 13	—	—	r = .34
				Stanford Achievement Test Social Studies score	F < 2.0 df = 1, 13	—	—	r = .46
Torrance & Parent (1966)	2 semesters	7-12	Flanders I/D Ratio	Sequential tests of educational progress, mathematics gain score	rho = .32	.184	3.3856	r = .32
Allen (1970)	2 semesters	1	Record of verbal behavior (developed from OScAR 4 V warmth score)	Number attainment test	(see Rosenshine, 1971, p. 79, since not presented in Allen's report.)	.83	.3727	r = −.23
				Number extension test	ditto	.83	.3727	r = −.23
				Number concepts test	ditto	.79	.4714	r = −.19
Soar (1966)	2 semesters	3-6	Rotated Factor 8: Indirectness vs. silence and confusion	Iowa Test of Basic Skills: Vocabulary	r = .068	.322	2.2664	r = .068
				Reading	r = .021	.443	1.6284	r = .021
				Arithmetic Concepts	r = .034	.408	1.7930	r = .034
				Arithmetic Problems	r = .083	.309	2.3488	r = .083
				Arithmetic Total	r = .081	.314	2.3167	r = .081

TABLE A Continued

Study	Duration of Teaching	Grade Level	No. of Teachers	Definition of Independent Variable	Definition of Dependent Variable	Result	Probability of Result	χ^2	Equivalent r Obtained by Glass et al. (1977)
Soar et al. (1971)	6 months	kinder-garten	35	Factor I: Free choice vs. struc-tured learning in groups	Lee-Clark Reading Readiness Test, 1/3 of original test	$r = .00$	.500	1.3863	$r = .00$
	6 months	1	20	Same as for kindergarten	Metropolitan Readiness Tests, 1/3 original length	$r = .30$	.099	4.6253	$r = .30$
Hunter (1968)	2 semesters	ages 8–14	11	Withall Scale: I/D Ratio similar to Flanders	Wide Range Achieve-ment Test: Median score on reading, spelling, and arithmetic	$r = .62$	.021	7.7265	$r = .62$
LaShier (1967)	6 weeks	8	10	Flanders I/D Ratio	Biological Sciences Curriculum Study Unit Test	tau = .60	.008	9.6566	$r = .60$
Pinney (1969)	Two 45-minute lessons	8–9	32[c]	Percentage of times teacher followed a pupil response with two or more rein-forcing statements (equivalent to "extended indirect-ness" in Flanders)	Achievement tests in social studies and English	$F = 4.2$ $df = 1, 30$	.170	3.5439	$r = .22$

aNote that, in this study, student achievement became the independent variable.

bThe Flanders system of interaction analysis was . . . used. From the observational data collected, percentage matrices were built from which scores for each teacher were extracted to form multivariate composite scores. These were: i/d Ratio, the ratio of motivating to controlling teacher behaviors; i/d Rows 8 and 9, which is similar to the i/d Ratio except that it only includes teacher response to pupil talk; extended i/d Ratio, which is similar to those above except that it examines extended motivation or control; 9–3 Cell, which represents the number of times the teacher accepted and used pupils' ideas, as shown on the matrix; 9–9 Cell representing extended pupil talk about their own ideas; and the 3–3 Cell, which represents teacher extension of pupils' ideas for some time.

c16 most and 16 least effective (as defined by adjusted student achievement) out of 56 teachers.

TABLE B
Teacher Indirectness and Student Achievement: Field Surveys; Alternative Findings for Three Methods of Combining Results Shown in Table A

Study	Most Significant Chi Squares	Mean Chi Squares	Least Significant Chi Squares
Flanders (1970) Grade 2	1.0051	1.0051	1.0051
Flanders (1970) Grade 4	4.1911	4.1911	4.1911
Flanders (1970) Grade 6	3.9039	3.9039	3.9039
Flanders (1970) Grade 7	6.7048	6.7048	6.7048
Flanders (1970) Grade 8	6.0319	6.0319	6.0319
Cook (1967)	5.4061	3.8391	3.0557
Furst (1967)	7.4594	7.4594	7.4594
Medley & Mitzel (1959)	5.0266	5.0266	5.0266
Powell (1968)[a]	—	—	—
Snider (1966)	3.7287	2.0578	1.3863
Soar (1966)	2.3488	2.0706	1.6284
Soar et al. (1971)	4.6253	3.0058	1.3863
Hunter (1968)	7.7265	7.7265	7.7265
LaShier (1965)	9.6566	9.6566	9.6566
Pinney (1969)	3.5439	3.5439	3.5439
Weber (1968)[a]	—	—	—
Thompson & Bowers (1968)[a]	—	—	—
Torrance & Parent (1966)	3.3856	3.3856	3.3856
Allen (1970)	.4714	.4056	.3727
Sum of Chi Squares	75.2157	70.0143	66.4648
Probability of Combined Result*	$p < .001$	$p < .001$	$p < .001$

*$\chi^2 (df = 32, p = .001) = 62.487$
[a]Data omitted because the significance test was based on the pupil as the unit of analysis.

TABLE C
Teacher Praise and Pupil Attitudes (Based on Dunkin and Biddle, 1974, p. 122)

Study	Duration of Teaching	Grade Level	No. of Teachers	Definition of Independent Variable	Definition of Dependent Variable	Result	Probability of Result	x^2
Flanders (1970)	2 semesters	2	15	Column 2—Flanders Interaction Analysis System (Teacher praise)	Average scores on a pupil attitude inventory	$r = .076$	.395	1.8577
Flanders (1970)	2 weeks	4	16	Column 2—Flanders Interaction Analysis System (Teacher praise)	Average scores on a pupil attitude inventory	$r = .397$	.069	5.3473
Flanders (1970)	2 semesters	6	30	Column 2—Flanders Interaction Analysis System (Teacher praise)	Average scores on a pupil attitude inventory	$r = .351$	.100	4.6052
Flanders (1970)	2 weeks	7	15	Column 2—Flanders Interaction Analysis System (Teacher praise)	Average scores on a pupil attitude inventory	$r = -.339$	.891	.2286
Flanders (1970)	2 weeks	8	16	Column 2—Flanders Interaction Analysis System (Teacher praise)	Average scores on a pupil attitude inventory	$r = .377$	.085	4.9302
							Sum of Chi Squares	16.9690
							Probability of Combined Result	$p < .10$

$x^2 (df = 10, p = .10) = 15.987$
$x^2 (df = 10, p = .05) = 18.307$

TABLE D
Teacher Acceptance of Pupils' Ideas and Pupil Achievement (Based on Dunkin and Biddle, 1974, p. 124)

Study	Duration of Teaching	Grade Level	No. of Teachers	Definition of Independent Variable	Definition of Dependent Variable	Result	Probability of Result	x^2
Flanders (1970)	2 semesters	2	15	Flanders Interaction Analysis Categories Sustained acceptance (3–3 cell)	"Portions of a nationally standardized achievement test covering language and number skills were used to form a composite score" (p. 393)	$r = -.450$	.953	.0963
Flanders (1970)	2 weeks	4	16	Flanders Interaction Analysis Categories Sustained acceptance (3–3 cell)	Achievement test covering a two-week unit	$r = .191$	.228	2.9568
Flanders (1970)	2 semesters	6	30	Flanders Interaction Analysis Categories Sustained acceptance (3–3 cell)	Same as for grade 2	$r = .303$	.072	5.2622
Flanders (1970)	2 weeks	7	15	Flanders Interaction Analysis Categories Sustained acceptance (3–3 cell)	Same as for grade 4	$r = .395$	.069	5.3473
Flanders (1970)	2 weeks	8	16	Flanders Interaction Analysis Categories Sustained acceptance (3–3 cell)	same as for grade 4	$r = .193$	.228	2.9568

Soar (1966)	2 semesters	3–6	55	Factor 8: Indirect Teaching vs. Silence and Confusion (Highest loadings were on "Extended indirect teacher influence," "Extended teacher elaboration of student idea," and "Teacher elaboration of student idea")	Iowa Test of Basic Skills (ITBS)			
					ITBS–Vocabulary	r = .068	.322	2.2664
					ITBS–Reading	r = .021	.443	1.6284
					ITBS–Arithmetic Concepts	r = .034	.408	1.7930
					ITBS–Arithmetic Problems	r = .083	.309	2.3488
					ITBS–Arithmetic Total	r = .081	.314	2.3167
Wright & Nuthall (1970)	Three 10-minute lessons	3	17	Teacher Behavior Inventory Category IV (Teacher Reaction to Pupil Response), Item 24 (Repetition of Pupil Response)	25-item Achievement test on the Black-backed gull	r = .17	.257	2.7174
Hughes (1973)	Three 40-minute lessons	7	1[a]	Teacher reaction categories: reacting vs. no reacting group	222-item achievement test on the exotic game animals of New Zealand	F = 8.889 df = 1, 57	.002	12.4292
Perkins (1965)	2 semesters	5	27	Factor III (Teacher Loading Recitation), Item 3 (Teacher uses Student's Idea)	California Achievement Tests Subtests: Reading Vocabulary, Arithmetic Reasoning, Arithmetic Fundamentals, Spelling	Factor Loading for Underachievers = .52; for Achievers = .49; no probability estimate made		

[a]One teacher taught 2 classes, using each of 2 methods with half of the students in each class.

TABLE E
Teacher Acceptance of Pupils' Ideas and Pupil Achievement: Alternative
Findings for Three Methods of Combining the Results Shown in Table D

Study	Most Significant Chi Squares	Mean Chi Squares	Least Significant Chi Squares
Flanders (1970) Grade 2	.0963	.0963	.0963
Flanders (1970) Grade 4	2.9568	2.9568	2.9568
Flanders (1970) Grade 6	5.2622	5.2622	5.2622
Flanders (1970) Grade 7	5.3473	5.3473	5.3473
Flanders (1970) Grade 8	2.9568	2.9568	2.9568
Soar (1966)	2.3488	2.0706	1.6284
Wright & Nuthall (1970)	2.7174	2.7174	2.7174
Hughes (1973)	12.4292	12.4292	12.4292
Perkins (1965)	—	—	—
Sum of Chi Squares	34.1148	33.8366	33.3944
Probability of Combined Result	$p < .01$	$p < .01$	$p < .01$

$x^2 (df = 16, p = .01) = 32.000$
$x^2 (df = 16, p = .001) = 39.252$

TABLE F
Teacher Criticism and Disapproval and Student Achievement (Based on Dunkin and Biddle, 1974, p. 126)

Study	Duration of Teaching	Grade Level	No. of Teachers	Definition of Independent Variable	Definition of Dependent Variable	Result	Probability of Result	x^2
Anthony (1967)	1 semester	5	21	Intensity of observed negative support (Process Characteristic 43) as measured by a rating scale	Stanford Achievement Test (median of six subtests)	$r = -.439$	.023	7.5445
Cook (1967)	2 semesters	10	8	Flanders Interaction Analysis System 1) Criticism (column 7)	Watson-Glaser Critical Thinking Appraisal Test; Processes of Science Test; Biological Science Curriculum Study Comprehensive Final Exam	Criticism median rho = -.33	.195	3.2695
				2) Extended criticism (cell 7-7)		Extended Criticism median rho = -.33	.195	3.2695
Flanders (1970)	2 semesters	2	15	Flanders Interaction Analysis Categories 1) Restrictiveness (cols. 6, 7)	"Portions of a nationally standardized achievement test covering language and number skills were used to form a composite score" (p. 393)	$r = -.100$	.361	2.0378
				2) Negative Authority $\left[\begin{array}{c}(6-7)\\+(7-6)\end{array}\right]$ cells		$r = .053$	.574	1.1103
				3) Restrictive Feedback $\left[(8-6)+(8-7)+(9-6)+(9-7)\right]$		$r = .175$	.738	.6076
Flanders (1970)	2 weeks	4	16	ditto	Achievement test covering two-week unit	$r = -.236$ $r = -.227$ $r = -.338$	.190 .199 .099	3.3215 3.2289 4.6253
Flanders (1970)	2 semesters	6	30	ditto	Same as for grade 2	$r = -.042$ $r = -.145$ $r = -.320$	.421 .245 .049	1.7302 2.8130 6.0319
Flanders (1970)	2 weeks	7	15	ditto	Same as for grade 4	$r = -.606$ $r = -.620$ $r = -.498$	.008 .007 .028	9.6566 9.9237 7.1511

TABLE F Continued

Study	Duration of Teaching	Grade Level	No. of Teachers	Definition of Independent Variable	Definition of Dependent Variable	Result	Probability of Result	x^2
Flanders (1970)	2 weeks	8	16	ditto	Same as for grade 4	$r = -.342$ $r = -.251$ $r = -.433$	.097 .174 .049	4.6661 3.4974 6.0319
Harris & Serwer (1966) (CRAFT-1)	2 semesters	1	48	Negative motivational statements as measured by OScAR-R	Stanford Achievement Test (SAT): SAT–Word Reading SAT–Paragraph Meaning SAT–Vocabulary SAT–Spelling SAT–Word Study Skills	$r = +.23$ $r = +.16$ $r = +.06$ $r = +.29$ $r = +.07$	.943 .864 .659 .978 .683	.1174 .2924 .8341 .0445 .7625
Harris et al., (1968) (CRAFT-2)	2 semesters	2	38	Same as CRAFT-1	Metropolitan Achievement Tests (MAT): MAT–Word Knowledge MAT–Word Discrimination MAT–Reading MAT–Spelling	$r = -.26$ $r = -.23$ $r = -.40$ $r = -.09$	.069 .095 .012 .301	5.3473 4.7078 8.8457 2.4013
Hunter (1968)	2 semesters	Emotionally Handicapped Ages 8–14	11	Revised Withall Categories 5) Directive statements related to school 6a) Neutral or mild disapproval 6b) Hostile or strong disapproval	Wide Range Achievement Tests (WRAT): Total Score on reading, spelling, arithmetic ditto ditto	median $r = -.61$ median $r = -.21$ median r across 3 subtests = -.23	.023 .268 .248	7.5445 2.6335 2.7887

Study				Variable	Test	median r		
Morsh (1956)	7 hours	Airmen	106	7) Teacher justification of authority	ditto	r = -.38	.125	4.1589
				Specially developed Observation Check-List. Instructor Verbal Behavior Category: Threatens or warns	Special test in aircraft hydraulics	r = .05	.689	.7450
Soar (1966)	2 semesters	3-6	55	Factor I—Teacher Criticism	Iowa Test of Basic Skills			
					ITBS: Vocabulary	r = -.16	.135	4.0050
					ITBS: Reading	r = -.128	.191	3.3110
					ITBS: Arithmetic Concepts	r = -.294	.019	7.9266
					ITBS: Arithmetic Problems	r = -.337	.009	9.4211
					ITBS: Arithmetic Total	r = -.362	.005	10.5966
Soar et al. (1971)	6 months	Kindergarten	35	Factor 4—Teacher Negative Affect vs. Pupil Work and Socialization with Adults	Lee-Clark Reading Readiness Test—1/3 of original test	r = -.10	.288	2.4896
	6 months	1	20	Same as for Kindergarten	Metropolitan Reading Tests, 1/3 original length	r = .12	.691	.7392
Spaulding (1965)	2 semesters	4, 6	21	Components of teacher-pupil transaction. Component 2: "Dominative through use of shame, ridicule, & threat." Component 10: "Formal group instruction with control through shame, ridicule, or admonition." Measured with the *Transaction Sample: Classroom (TSC)*	Sequential Tests of Educational Progress			
					STEP—Component 2 (reading)	r = -.49	.012	8.8457
					STEP—Component 2 (mathematics)	r = -.10	.333	2.1992
					STEP—Component 10 (reading)	r = -.42	.029	7.0809
					STEP—Component 10 (mathematics)	r = -.08	.365	2.0157

TABLE F Continued

Study	Duration of Teaching	Grade Level	No. of Teachers	Definition of Independent Variable	Definition of Dependent Variable	Result	Probability of Result	χ^2
Wallen (1966)	2 semesters	1	36	Total percentage of teacher behavior in modified Flanders' Category 7: Personal Control	California Achievement Test			
					CAT–Reading Vocabulary	$r = -.379$	.031	6.9475
					CAT–Reading Comprehension	$r = -.136$	.259	2.7019
					CAT–Arithmetic	$r = -.220$	.146	3.8483
Wallen (1966)	2 semesters	3	40	ditto	CAT–Reading Vocabulary	$r = -.226$	.060	5.6268
				ditto	CAT–Reading Comprehension	$r = -.219$	.097	4.6661
				ditto	CAT–Vocabulary	$r = -.144$	.160	3.6652
Wright & Nuthall (1970)	Three 10-minute lessons	3	17	Teacher reaction to pupil response 1) Item 22–Managerial Comment	25-item achievement test on Black-backed gull	$r = -.22$	.199	3.2289
				2) Item 23–Challenging Comment	ditto	$r = -.38$	.067	5.4061

TABLE G
Teacher Criticism and Disapproval and Student Achievement: Alternative Findings for Three Methods of Combining Results Shown in Table F

Study	Most Significant Chi Squares	Mean Chi Squares	Least Significant Chi Squares
Anthony (1967)	7.5445	7.5445	7.5445
Cook (1967)	3.2695	3.2695	3.2695
Flanders (1970) Grade 2	2.0378	1.2519	.6076
Flanders (1970) Grade 4	4.6253	3.7252	3.2289
Flanders (1970) Grade 6	6.0319	3.5250	1.7302
Flanders (1970) Grade 7	9.9237	8.9104	7.1511
Flanders (1970) Grade 8	6.0319	4.7318	3.4974
Hunter (1968)	7.5445	4.2814	2.6335
Soar (1966)	10.5966	7.0520	3.3110
Wright & Nuthall (1970)	5.4061	4.3175	3.2289
Wallen (1966)	6.9475	4.4992	2.7019
Wallen (1966)	5.6268	4.6527	3.6652
Spaulding (1965)	8.8457	5.0353	2.0157
Harris & Serwer (1966)	.8341	.4101	.0445
Harris et al. (1968)	8.8457	5.3255	2.4013
Morsh (1956)	.7450	.7450	.7450
Soar et al. (1971)	2.4896	1.6144	.7392
Sum of Chi Squares	97.3462	70.8914	48.5154
Probability of Combined Result	$p < .001$	$p < .001$	$p < .10$

$x^2 (df = 34, p = .10) = 44.903$
$x^2 (df = 34, p = .05) = 48.602$
$x^2 (df = 34, p = .02) = 52.995$
$x^2 (df = 34, p = .01) = 56.061$
$x^2 (df = 34, p = .001) = 65.247$

REFERENCES

NOTE: Numbers in brackets at the end of a reference indicate the pages of this book on which the reference is cited.

Allen, G. *The relationship between certain aspects of teachers' verbal behaviour and the number development of their pupils.* Paper presented at the Founding Conference of the Australian Association for Research in Education, Sydney, 1970. [99, 102]

American Institutes for Research. *Impact of educational innovation on student performance: Project methods and findings for three cohorts* (Project LONG-STEP Final Report: Volume 1). Executive Summary. Palo Alto, Cal.: American Institutes for Research, 1976. [33]

Anthony, B. C. M. *The identification and measurement of classroom environmental process variables related to academic achievement.* Unpublished doctoral dissertation, University of Chicago, 1967. [107, 111]

Barber, T. X. *Pitfalls in human research: Ten pivotal points.* New York: Pergamon, 1976. [87]

Beavin, J. C. H. *Interpersonal judgment and performance control.* Unpublished doctoral dissertation, Stanford University, 1970. [80]

Bell, A. E.; Zipursky, M. A.; & Switzer, F. Informal or open-area education in relation to achievement and personality. *British Journal of Educational Psychology,* 1976, *46,* 235–243. [32]

Bellack, A. A.; Hyman, R. T.; Smith, F. L., Jr.; & Kliebard, H. M. *The language of the classroom.* New York: Teachers College Press, 1966. [23]

Bennett, N.; with Jordon, J.; Long, G.; & Wade, B. *Teaching styles and pupil progress.* Cambridge, Mass.: Harvard University Press, 1976. [34–35]

Berliner, D. C. *Instructional time in research on teaching.* Paper presented at the meetings of the American Educational Research Association, April 1977. San Francisco: Far West Laboratory for Educational Research and Development, 1977. (Mimeographed) [74]

Berliner, D. C.; Cahen, L. S.; Filby, N.; Fisher, C.; Marliave, R.; & Moore, J. *Proposal for Phase III-B of the Beginning Teacher Evaluation Study. July 1, 1976-June 30, 1978.* San Francisco: Far West Laboratory for Educational Research and Development, 1976. [40]

Blumer, H. *Symbolic interactionism*. Englewood Cliffs, N.J.: Prentice-Hall, 1969. [66]

Borg, W. R. The minicourse as a vehicle for changing teaching behavior. *Journal of Educational Psychology*, 1972, *63*, 572–579. [49, 60]

Borg, W. R.; Kelley, M. L.; Langer, Philip; & Gall, Meredith. *The minicourse: A microteaching approach to teacher education*. Beverly Hills, Cal.: Macmillan Educational Services, 1970. [49]

Bozarth, J. D., & Roberts, R. R., Jr. Signifying significant significance. *American Psychologist*, 1972, *27*, 774–775. [28]

Brophy, J., & Evertson, C. *The Texas Teacher Effectiveness Study: Classroom coding manual* (Research Report No. 76–2). Austin: Research and Development Center for Teacher Education, University of Texas, 1973. [36]

Brophy, J. E., & Evertson, C. M. *Process-product correlations in the Texas Teacher Effectiveness Study: Final Report* (Research Report No. 74–4). Austin: Research and Development Center for Teacher Education, University of Texas, 1974. [36–37, 38]

Bruner, J. S. Foreword. In N. Bennett et al., *Teaching styles and pupil progress*. Cambridge, Mass.: Harvard University Press, 1976. [34]

Burns, M. L. The effects of feedback and commitment to change on the behavior of elementary school principals. *Journal of Applied Behavioral Science*, 1977, *13*, 159–166. [51]

Calfee, R. C. Personal communication. March 1976. [67]

Centra, J. A. Effectiveness of student feedback in modifying college instruction. *Journal of Educational Psychology*, 1973, *65*, 395–401. [51]

Clark, D. C. Teaching concepts in the classroom: A set of teaching prescriptions derived from experimental research. *Journal of Educational Psychology*, 1971, *62*, 253–278. (Monograph) [46]

Clifford, G. J. A history of the impact of research on teaching. In R. M. W. Travers (Ed.), *Second handbook of research on teaching*. Chicago: Rand McNally, 1973. [43]

Committee on the Criteria of Teacher Effectiveness, American Educational Research Association. Report of the Committee. *Review of Educational Research*, 1952, *22*, 238–263. [24]

Conant, J. B. *The education of American teachers*. New York: McGraw-Hill, 1963. [42]

Cook, R. E. *The effect of teacher methodology upon certain achievements of students in secondary school biology*. Unpublished doctoral dissertation, University of Iowa, 1967. [97, 102, 107, 111]

Cook, T. D., & Campbell, D. T. The design and conduct of quasi-experiments and true experiments in field settings. In M. D. Dunnette (Ed.), *Handbook of industrial and organizational psychology*. Chicago: Rand McNally, 1976. [87]

Crawford, J., & Gage, N. L. Development of a research-based teacher education program. *California Journal of Teacher Education*, 1977, *4*, 105–123. [18]

Cronbach, L. J., & Snow, R. E. *Aptitudes and instructional methods: A handbook for research on interactions*. New York: Irvington, 1977. [79]

Cunningham, W. G. (Ed.). Technology and education. *Phi Delta Kappan*, 1977, *58*, 450–467. [14]

Daw, R. W., & Gage, N. L. Effect of feedback from teachers to principals. *Journal of Educational Psychology*, 1967, *58*, 181–188. [51]

Domino, G. Interactive effects of achievement orientation and teaching style on academic achievement. *Journal of Educational Psychology*, 1971, *62*, 427–431. [79]

Doyle, W. Paradigms for research on teacher effectiveness. In L. S. Shulman (Ed.), *Review of research in education* (Vol. 5). Itasca, Ill.: F. E. Peacock, 1978. [69–74]

Dubin, R., & Taveggia, T. C. *The teaching-learning paradox: A comparative analysis of college teaching methods*. Eugene: Center for the Advanced Study of Educational Administration, University of Oregon, 1968. [27]

Dunkin, M. J., & Biddle, B. J. *The study of teaching*. New York: Holt, Rinehart & Winston, 1974. [22, 23, 25–26, 28, 29, 84]

Eisner, E. W. On the uses of educational connoisseurship and criticism for evaluating classroom life. *Teachers College Record*, 1977, *78*, 345–358. [15, 16]

Elstein, A. S. Clinical judgment: Psychological research and medical practice. *Science*, 1976, *194*, 676–700. [17]

Faw, H. W., & Waller, T. G. Mathemagenic behaviors and efficiency in learning from prose materials: Review, critique, and recommendations. *Review of Educational Research*, 1976, *46*, 691–720. [60]

Feiman, Sharon, Evaluating teacher centers. *School Review*, 1977, *85*, 395–411. [58]

Fisher, C. W.; Filby, N. N.; & Marliave, R. S. *Instructional time and student achievement in second grade reading and mathematics*. Paper presented at the meetings of the American Educational Research Association, April 1977. San Francisco: Far West Laboratory for Educational Research and Development, 1977. (Mimeographed) [75, 78]

Flanders, N. A. Teacher influence in the classroom. In E. J. Amidon & J. B. Hough (Eds.), *Interaction analysis: Theory, research and application*. Reading, Mass.: Addison-Wesley, 1967. [25–26]

Flanders, N. A. *Analyzing teacher behavior*. Reading, Mass.: Addison-Wesley, 1970. [50, 96, 102, 103, 104, 106, 107–108, 111]

Flexner, A. *Medical education in the United States and Canada. Bulletin No. 4.* New York: Carnegie Foundation for the Advancement of Teaching, 1910. [43]

Friedlander, B. Z. Some remarks on "open education." *American Educational Research Journal*, 1975, *12*, 465–468. [32]

Furst, N. F. *The multiple languages of the classroom*. Paper presented at the annual meeting of the American Educational Research Association, New York, 1967. [97, 102]

Gage, N. L. Paradigms for research on teaching. In N. L. Gage (Ed.), *Handbook of research on teaching*. Chicago: Rand McNally, 1963. [69]

Gage N. L. *Teacher effectiveness and teacher education*. Palo Alto, Cal.: Pacific Books, 1972. [76]

Gage, N. L. (Ed.). *The psychology of teaching methods: The 75th Yearbook of the National Society for the Study of Education, Part I.* Chicago: Universiy of Chicago Press, 1976. [76]

Gage, N.L., & Berliner D. C. *Educational psychology.* Chicago: Rand McNally, 1975. [75]

Gage,N. L.; Runkel, P. J.; & Chatterjee, B. B. Changing teacher behavior through feedback from pupils: An application of equilibrium theory. In W. W. Charters, Jr., & N. L. Gage (Eds.), *Readings in the social psychology of education.* Boston: Allyn & Bacon, 1963. [51]

Gagné, R. M. The learning basis of teaching methods. In N. L. Gage (Ed.), *The psychology of teaching methods: The 75th Yearbook of the National Society for the Study of Education, Part I.* Chicago: University of Chicago Press, 1976. [76]

Gall, M. D.; Ward, B. A.; Berliner, D. C.; Cahen, L. A.; Crown, K. A.; Elashoff, J. D.; Stanton, G. C.; & Winne, P. H. *The effects of teacher use of questioning techniques on student achievement and attitudes. Vol. 1, Final Report* (HEW Contract No. NE–C–00–3–0108). San Francisco: Far West Laboratory for Educational Research and Development, March 1976. [59]

Garfield, Eugene. Negative science and "the outlook for the flying machine." *Current Contents: Social and Behavioral Sciences,* 1977, *9* (26), 5–16. [92]

Gergen, K. J. Social psychology as history. *Journal of Personality and Social Psychology,* 1973, *26,* 309–320. [19]

Glaser, Robert. *Adaptive education: Individual diversity and learning.* New York: Holt, Rinehart & Winston, 1977. [78–79]

Glass, G. V . *Primary, secondary, and meta-analysis of research.* Presidential address presented at the 1976 Annual Meeting of the American Educational Research Association. Boulder: Laboratory of Educational Research, University of Colorado, 1976. (Multilith) [25, 28]

Glass, Gene V . Integrating findings: The meta-analysis of research. In L. S. Shulman (Ed.), *Review of Research in Education,* (Vol.5). Itasca, Ill.: F. E. Peacock, 1978. [30]

Glass, G. V; Coulter, Diane; Hartley, Susan; Hearold, Susan; Kahl, Stuart; Kalk, John; & Sherretz, Lynn. *Teacher "indirectness" and pupil achievement: An integration of findings.* Boulder: Laboratory of Educational Research, University of Colorado, 1977. (Multilith) [30–31]

Gliessman, D., & Pugh, R. C. The development and evaluation of protocol films of teacher behavior. *AVCR (Audio-Visual Communications Review),* 1976, *24* (1), 21–48. [45]

Golladay, M. A. *The condition of education: 1977 edition, A statistical report on the condition of education in the United States, Vol. 3, Part 1.* Washington, D.C.: National Center for Education Statistics, U. S. Department of Health, Education, and Welfare, 1977. [13]

Good, T. L. Review of *Teaching styles and pupil progress* by N. Bennett (with J. Jordan, G. Long, & B. Wade). *Journal of Curriculum Studies,* 1977, *8,* 183–186. [34]

Good, T. L.; Biddle, B. J.; & Brophy, J. E. *Teachers make a difference.* New York: Holt, Rinehart & Winston, 1975. [24]

Good, T. L., & Brophy, J. E. Changing teacher and student behavior: An empirical investigation. *Journal of Educational Psychology,* 1974, *66,* 390–405. [51]

Goodlad, J. I. What goes on in our schools? *Educational Researcher,* 1977, *6* (3), 3–6. [41]

Gray, J., & Satterly, D. A chapter of errors: Teaching styles and pupil progress in retrospect. *Educational Research,* 1976, *19* (1), 45–56. [35]

Greer, W. D. *The criticism of teaching.* Unpublished doctoral dissertation, Stanford University, 1973. [15]

Guthrie, J. T., & Seifert, Mary. Letter-sound complexity in learning to identify words. *Journal of Educational Psychology,* 1977, *69,* 686–696.[77]

Harris, A. J.; Morrison, C.; Serwer, B. L.; & Gold, L. *A continuation of the CRAFT Project: Comparing reading approaches with disadvantaged urban Negro children in primary grades* (USOE Project No. 5–0570–2–12–1). New York: Division of Teacher Education, City University of New York, 1968. [108, 111]

Harris, A. J., & Serwer, B. L. *Comparison of reading approaches in first grade teaching with disadvantaged children (the CRAFT Project)* (USOE Cooperative Research Project No. 2677). New York: City University of New York, 1966. [108, 111]

Hart, W. A. Is teaching what the philosopher understands by it? *British Journal of Educational Studies,* 1976, *24* (2), 155–170. [13]

Heath, R. W., & Nielson, M. A. The research basis for performance-based teacher education. *Review of Educational Research,* 1974, *44,* 463–483. [24, 64]

Hedges, Larry V. A meta-analysis of studies of four teacher behavior variables. Stanford, Cal.: The author, School of Education, Stanford University, 1977. [24]

Hersen, M., & Barlow, D. H. *Single-case experimental designs: Strategies for studying behavior change.* New York: Pergamon, 1976. [89]

Hillis, J. W., & Wortman, C. B. Some determinants of public acceptance of randomized control group experimental designs. *Sociometry* (in press). [86]

Holton, G. On the role of themata in scientific thought. *Science,* 1975, *188,* 328–338. [19]

Hovenier, P. J. *Changing the behavior of social studies department heads through the use of feedback.* Unpublished doctoral dissertation, Stanford University, 1966. [51]

Hudgins, B. B. *Self-contained training materials for teacher education: A derivation from research on the learning of complex skills.* Bloomington: National Center for the Development of Training Materials in Teacher Education, Indiana University, 1974. (Multilith) [46]

Hughes, D. C. An experimental investigation of the effects of pupil responding and teacher reacting on pupil achievement. *American Educational Research Journal,* 1973, *10* (1), 21–37. [105, 106]

Hunt, K. Do we really need more replications? *Psychological Reports,* 1975, *36,* 587–593. [28]

Hunter, C. P. *Classroom climate and pupil characteristics in special classes for the educationally handicapped*. Unpublished doctoral dissertation, University of Southern California, 1968. [100, 102, 108, 111]

Jones, L. V., & Fiske, D. W. Models for testing the significance of combined results. *Psychological Bulletin*, 1953, *50*, 375–381. [29]

Kazdin, A. E. Statistical analyses for single-case experimental designs. In Michael Hersen & D. H. Barlow, *Single-case experimental designs: Strategies for studying behavior change*. New York: Pergamon, 1976. Pp. 265–316. [89]

Kemble, Eugenia. Why teachers want teacher centers. *New York Teacher, Magazine Section*, November 11, 1973. [57]

Kiesler, S. B., & Turner, C. F. (Eds.). *Fundamental research and the process of education: Final report of the committee on fundamental research relevant to education*. Washington, D.C.: National Academy of Sciences, 1977. [93]

King, J. C.; Hayes, P. C.; & Newman, Isadore. Some requirements for successful inservice education. *Phi Delta Kappan*, 1977, *58*, 686–687. [43]

Klausmeier, H. J.; Ghatala, E. S.; & Frayer, D. A. *Conceptual learning and development: A cognitive view*. New York: Academic Press, 1974. [77]

Koerner, J. D. *The miseducation of American teachers*. Boston: Houghton Mifflin, 1963. [42]

Kuhn, T. S. *The structure of scientific revolutions*. Chicago: University of Chicago Press, 1962. [93]

LaShier, W. S. *An analysis of certain aspects of the verbal behavior of student teachers of eighth grade students participating in a BSCS laboratory block*. Unpublished doctoral dissertation, University of Texas, 1965. [100, 102]

Lilienthal, A. M.; Pedersen, E.; & Dowd, J. E. *Cancer epidemiology: Methods of study*. Baltimore: Johns Hopkins Press, 1967. [21]

LoPresti, Peter L. California: The impact of the Commission for Teacher Preparation and Licensing. *Phi Delta Kappan*, 1977, *58*, 674–677. [43]

MacLeod, Gordon, & McIntyre, Donald. Towards a model for microteaching. *British Journal of Teacher Education*, 1977, *3*, 111–120. [48]

Majasan, J. K. *College students' achievement as a function of the congruence between their beliefs and their instructor's beliefs*. Unpublished doctoral dissertation, Stanford University, 1972. [79]

Markle, S. M. (Chair). *Bidecennial afterthoughts on the teaching machine, 1956–1976*. Symposium at the American Psychological Association Annual Convention, September 6, 1976. [43]

McClure, R. M. *Pilot project on practitioner selection, use and critique of in-service education products. Vol. I, Review of project*. San Francisco: Far West Laboratory for Educational Research and Development, 1976. [55]

McDonald, F. J., & Elias, P. *The effects of teaching performance on pupil learning, Beginning Teacher Evaluation Study: Phase II, Final Report, Vol. I*. Princeton, N.J.: Educational Testing Service, 1976. [38, 90–91]

McGuire, W. J. The yin and yang of progress in social psychology: Seven koan. *Journal of Personality and Social Psychology*, 1973, *26*, 446–456. [90]

McKeachie, W. J. Psychology in America's bicentennial year. *American Psychologist*, 1976, *31*, 819–833. [52]

McKeachie, W. J., & Kulik, J. A. Effective college teaching. In F. N. Kerlinger (Ed.), *Review of research in education, Vol. 3.* Itasca, Ill.: F. E. Peacock, 1975. Pp. 165–209. [27]

McMurray, N. E.; Bernard, M. E.;Klausmeier, H. J.; Schilling, J. M.; & Vorwerk, K. Instructional design for accelerating children's concept learning. *Journal of Educational Psychology,* 1977, *69,* 660–667. [77]

Medley, D.M. *Teacher competence and teacher effectiveness: A review of process-product research.* Washington, D.C.: American Association of Colleges for Teacher Education, 1977. [31, 35, 38, 39]

Medley, D. M., & Mitzel, H. E. Some behavioral correlates of teacher effectivenss. *Journal of Educational Psychology,* 1959, *50,* 239–246. [97, 102]

Messerli, Jonathan. Building the bridge before we can cross it. *Phi Delta Kappan,* 1977, *58,* 667–670. [43]

Mitzel, H. E. Teacher effectiveness. In C. W. Harris (Ed.) *Encyclopedia of educational research* (3rd ed.). New York: Macmillan, 1960. [22]

Morsh, J. B. *Systematic observation of instructor behavior.* Lackland Air Force Base, San Antonio, Texas: USAF Personnel Training Research Center (Development Report No. AFPTRC–TR–56–32), 1956. [109, 111]

Newcomb, Simon. The outlook for the flying machine. *The Independent: A Weekly Magazine,* October 22, 1903, pp. 2508–2512. Reprinted in *Current Contents: Social and Behavioral Sciences,* 1977, *9* (26), 17–22. [92]

Pepper, Stephen C. *The basis of criticism in the arts.* Cambridge, Mass.: Harvard University Press, 1945. [15]

Perkins, H. V. Classroom behavior and underachievement. *American Educational Research Journal,* 1965, *2,* 1–12. [105, 106]

Peterson, P. L. *Interactive effects of student anxiety, achievement orientation, and teacher behavior on student achievement and attitude.* Unpublished doctoral dissertation, Stanford University, 1976. [79]

Pinney, R. W. *Presentational behaviors related to success in teaching.* Unpublished doctoral dissertation, Stanford University, 1969. [100, 102]

Powell, E. R. *Teacher behavior and pupil achievement.* Paper presented at the annual meeting of the American Educational Research Association, Chicago, 1968. [100, 102]

Powell, J. L. After Lancaster: Some reflections on the progressive–traditional controversy. *Education: The newsletter of the Scottish Council for Research in Education,* 1976, *16,* 1–4. [34]

Program on Teaching Effectiveness, SCRDT. *Teacher training products: The state of the field* (R & D Memo No. 116). Stanford, Cal.: Stanford Center for Research and Development in Teaching, 1974. [53]

Program on Teaching Effectiveness, SCRDT. *A factorially designed experiment on teacher structuring, soliciting, and reacting* (R&D Memo No. 147). Stanford, Cal.: Stanford Center for Research and Development in Teaching, 1976. HEW Contract No. NE–C–00–3–0061. [59, 67]

Program on Teaching Effectiveness, CERAS. *An experiment on teacher effectiveness and parent-assisted instruction in the third grade, Vol. 1.* Stanford, Cal.: Center for Educational Research, Stanford University, 1977 (in press). [35, 36]

Reichenbach, Hans. *The rise of scientific philosophy*. Berkeley: University of California Press, 1951. [83]

Rist, R. C. On the relations among research paradigms: From disdain to détente. *Anthropology & Education Quarterly*, 1977, *8*, 42–49. [82, 83]

Rogers, V. R. (Ed.). Teachers centers. *Educational Leadership,* 1976, *33* (6), 1–180. [57]

Rogers, V., & Baron, J. Teaching styles and pupil progress. *Phi Delta Kappan*, 1977, *58*, 622–623. [34]

Röhr, G. Results on standardized achievement tests for students in grades 3 and 6: A comparative study of some open-plan schools and traditionally built schools in Malmö. *Didakometry and Sociometry*, 1976, *8* (1), 12. (Abstract only) [32]

Roland, J. On the reduction of "knowing that" to "knowing how." In B. O. Smith & R. H. Ennis (Eds.), *Language and concepts in education*. Chicago: Rand McNally, 1961. [45]

Rosenshine, Barak. *Teaching behaviours and student achievement*. London: National Foundation for Educational Research in England and Wales, 1971. [45]

Rosenshine, Barak. Classroom instruction. In N. L. Gage (Ed.), *The psychology of teaching methods: The 75th yearbook of the National Society for the Study of Education, Part 1*. Chicago: University of Chicago Press, 1976. [24, 35, 39, 59]

Rosenshine, Barak, & Furst, N. F. The use of direct observation to study teaching. In R. M. W. Travers (Ed.), *Second handbook of research on teaching*. Chicago: Rand McNally, 1973. [84]

Royce, J. Is there a science of education? *Educational Review*, 1891, *1*, 15–25, 121–132. Reprinted in M. L. Borrowman (Ed.), *Teacher education in America: A documentary history*. New York: Teachers College Press, 1965. Pp. 100–127. [20]

Ryan, K. (Ed.), *Teacher education: The 74th yearbook of the National Society for the Study of Education, Part II*. Chicago: University of Chicago Press, 1975. [42]

Ryle, G. *The concept of mind*. New York: Barnes & Noble, 1949. [44]

Shavelson, R., & Dempsey, N. Generalizability of measures of teaching behavior. *Review of Educational Research*, 1976, *46*, 553–611. [24]

Sidman, Murray. *Tactics of scientific research: Evaluating experimental data in psychology*. New York: Basic Books, 1960. [87]

Simon, A., & Boyer, E. G. (Eds.). *Mirrors for behavior III: An anthology of observation instruments* (new ed.). Wyncote, Pa.: Communication Materials Center, 1974. [84]

Snider, R. M. *A project to study the nature of effective physics teaching* (U.S. Office of Education Research Project No. S-280). Ithaca, N.Y.: Cornell University. Also available as an unpublished doctoral dissertation, Cornell University, 1966. [98, 102]

Soar, R. S. *An integrative approach to classroom learning* (Final Report, Public Health Service Grant No. 5–R11–MH 01096 & National Institute of Mental

Health Grant No. 7–R11–MH02045). Philadelphia: Temple University, 1966. [99, 102, 105, 106, 109, 111]

Soar, R. S. *Final report, Follow Through classroom process measurement and pupil growth (1970-1971)*. Gainesville: Institute for the Development of Human Resources, University of Florida, 1973. [38]

Soar, R. S.; Soar, R. M.; & Ragosta, M. *The validation of an observation system for classroom management*. Paper presented at the annual meeting of the American Educational Research Association, New York, 1971. [100, 102, 109, 111]

Spaulding, R. L. *Achievement, creativity, and self-concept correlates of teacher-pupil transactions in elementary schools* (U.S. Office of Education Cooperative Research Project No. 1352). New York: Hofstra University, 1965. [109, 111]

Spencer, R. L., & Boyd, W. E. CBTE is succeeding in the State of New York. *Phi Delta Kappan*, 1977, *58*, 677–679, 687. [43]

Stallings, Jane, & Kaskowitz, D. *Follow Through classroom observation evaluation, 1972-1973* (SRI Project URU–7370). Menlo Park, Cal.: Stanford Research Institute, 1974. [38, 67]

Sterling, T. C. Publication decisions and their possible effects on inferences drawn from tests of significance — or vice versa. *Journal of American Statistical Association*, 1959, *54* (No. 285), 30–34. [28]

Taveggia, T. C. Resolving research controversy through empirical cumulation: Toward reliable sociological knowledge. *Sociological Methods & Research*, 1974, *2*, 395–407. [25]

Thomas, Lewis. The future place of science in the art of healing. *Journal of Medical Education*, 1976, *51* (1), 23–29. [92]

Thompson, G. R., & Bowers, N. C. *Fourth grade achievement as related to creativity, intelligence, and teaching style*. Paper presented at the annual meeting of the American Educational Research Association, Chicago, 1968. [99, 102]

Thoresen, C. E., & Anton, J. L. Intensive experimental research in counseling. *Journal of Counseling Psychology*, 1974, *21*, 553–559. [87]

Thornbury, R. (Ed.). *Teachers' centres*. New York: Agathon Press, 1974. [57]

Tikunoff, W. J., & Ward, B. A. (Eds.). Special issue: Exploring qualitative–quantitative research methodologies in education. *Anthropology & Education Quarterly*, 1977, *8*, 37–163. [82]

Torrance, E. P., & Parent, E. *Characteristics of mathematics teachers that affect students' learning* (Cooperative Research Project No. 1020, U.S. Office of Education). Washington, D.C.: Office of Education, Department of Health, Education, and Welfare, 1966. [99, 102]

Traub, Ross; Weiss, Joel; Fisher, Charles; Musella, Donald; & Khan, Sar. *Openness in schools: An evaluation of the Wentworth County Roman Catholic School Board Schools*. Toronto: Educational Evaluation Center, Ontario Institute for Studies in Education, 1973. [31]

Travers, R. M. W., & Dillon, Jacqueline. *The making of a teacher: A plan for professional self-development*. New York: Macmillan, 1975. [52]

Trinchero, R. L., Jr. *Three technical skills of teaching: Their acquisition, stability, and effects on student performance*. Unpublished doctoral dissertation, Stanford University, 1975. [48]

Turney, C.; Clift, J. C.; Dunkin, M. J.; & Traill, R. D. *Microteaching: Research, theory and practice*. Sydney, Australia: Sydney University Press, 1973. [48]

Viehoever, Kent. *Some issues in social science methodology, with suggested resolutions: From détente toward integration*. Washington, D.C.: The author, National Institute of Education, 1976. (Unpublished draft) [82–83]

Wagner, A. C. Changing teacher behavior: A comparison of microteaching and cognitive discrimination training. *Journal of Educational Psychology*, 1973, *64*, 299–305. [50]

Wallace, J. M. The making of a profession: An Oregon case study. *Phi Delta Kappan*, 1977, *58*, 671–673. [43]

Wallen, N. E. *Relationships between teacher characteristics and student behavior, Part 3* (U.S. Office of Education Cooperative Research Project No. SAE OE5-10-181). Salt Lake City: University of Utah, 1966. [110, 111]

Ward, B. E. *A survey of microteaching in NCATE-accredited secondary education programs* (R&D Memo No. 70). Stanford, Cal.: Stanford Center for Research and Development in Teaching, 1970. [47]

Ward, W. D., & Barcher, P. R. Reading achievement and creativity as related to open classroom experience. *Journal of Educational Psychology*, 1975, *67*, 683–691. [32]

Weber, W. A. *Relationships between teacher behavior and pupil creativity in the elementary school*. Unpublished doctoral dissertation, Temple University, 1968. [98, 102]

Wright, C. J., & Nuthall, G. Relationships between teacher behaviors and pupil achievement in three experimental elementary science lessons. *American Educational Research Journal*, 1970, *7*, 477–491. [105, 106, 110, 111]

Wright, R. J. The affective and cognitive consequences of an open education elementary school. *American Educational Research Journal*, 1975, *12*, 449–568. [32]

Yin, R. K.; Bingham, Eveleen; & Heald, K. A. The difference that quality makes: The case of research reviews. *Sociological Methods & Research*, 1976, *5* (2), 139–156. [25]